GROW YOUR CASH FLOW

by
Ana Weber

STORY MERCHANT BOOKS
LOS ANGELES
2019

STORY MERCHANT BOOKS

ISBN: 978-1-970157-01-7

Story Merchant Books
400 S. Burnside Avenue #11B
Los Angeles, CA 90036

http://www.storymerchantbooks.com

Cover & interior formatting by IndieDesignz.com

DEDICATION

To my family, with love!

Contents

PREFACE

Although money is not life, it is both a metaphor for life and a tool to organize your life. And like other tools in our lives, our relationship with money can help us or hurt us. Using the lessons I've learned in my own journey around money, this book gives you many ways to turn money into a positive force in your life—whether or not you currently have a little or a lot of it. Money flows in and out of our lives, and back in again, along with flows around relationships, career, life passions, and special moments. *The Cash Flow* represents the flow of life. How money flows through and around you becomes an integral part of your life—but one you can influence, or even control.

To put it another way—whether you have a lot or a little, you can take charge of your relationship with money. By understanding that money is affected by human interaction, you can interact with other people in ways that create so much positivity, money starts flowing to you.

We live the life we choose to live, sometimes by following cold calculations, other times by going with our deep emotions, and most times moving in between those two extremes. Our decisions around money are also along this spectrum.

For myself, my two lifelong goals have been to achieve happiness and to help others. Money can certainly make these two goals easier, but it is not required. I was happy even when I was desperately poor, because I was helping others. And I am still happy now that I am financially well-off, because I don't let a desire for more and more money dictate my life. I strive to be a good person and a happy person, and the money I have is just another tool for this.

Ultimately, it is never about money—how much we have and how much we want. It is about the lives we touch in the process and how much we grow, acknowledge, admire, and appreciate in our lives—which, as a miraculous side effect, sends money flowing toward us. In this book, I share with you my life story and the cash flow in my life—how it began to come to me, what I have done and not done with it—as I have striven for (and mostly achieved) personal happiness and joyful state of mind.

Contentment is not easy to achieve or maintain. Life will throw us a rope sometimes, as we struggle to stay above big ocean waves. Other times, we have to swim across the ocean and feel every moment of the journey—but that makes the victory of reaching the other side even sweeter.

Either way, the journey itself is the key.

You've heard, "Do what you love, and the money will follow." Remember that it also works the other way: "*Love what you do*, and the money will follow." I send my love to you, wishing you a happy journey. Life is precious, and its most delicate and nourishing component is love. Never stop adding a dash of love to your daily diet!

I've been thinking about this book for a long time. It is thrilling to see it come to fruition, because I know my story—my personal journey from poverty to wealth—can guide you on your own path, even though your path will be different.

Please share this book with all your loved ones, so they can grow in their own relationships with money, and make positive changes in their own lives. They will thank you—and so do I.

Ana

PART I

Money Was My Enemy—
Now It's My Friend

Cash flow remains elusive
to so many of us.
But it doesn't have to be that way.

From grinding poverty as a Jewish child in post-World War II Romania to building a new and successful life first in Israel and then again in the United States, I've learned some incredible lessons about money. I have seen it come and go and come back again. In the process, I've learned to make money my friend and ally.

Because I'm passionate about revealing my relationship with money, I can't wait to share the many gifts my unique life history has given me. By showing you the triumphs and tragedies of my own experiences with money, I hope to make a difference in your life. Although your experiences and situations will be different than mine, the basic principles I've learned are universal; you can easily apply them in your own life.

Just the word *money* sets off such a variety of emotions in every one of us: fear, craving, dread... did I mention fear?

I finally came to grips with my own issues around money. I replaced a poverty mindset with a positive attitude and belief system—and this led me on a journey of increasing happiness, peace, and success for five decades.

In this book, I'll share my cash flow systems with you through personal anecdotes and solutions based on my relentless—and successful—search for a great life. It's been a very personal and emotional journey. While I've shed quite a few tears remembering where I started and what I have overcome, today I look back on all of it with unbridled joy. Life teaches such amazing lessons...if we're just willing to listen and learn.

CHAPTER 1

Epiphany at Age Eight: How Selling a Magazine to a Stranger Created a Lifelong Passion

Takeaway Tools:

- **Early Start.** Our earliest experiences shape us for the rest of our lives.
- **Kindness is Deep.** Simple acts of kindness can change a life in ways you never imagined.
- **Hollow Victories.** A victory based on throwing away your ethics is no victory at all.

In Cluj, Romania, the capital of Transylvania—where I was born—my parents divorced when I was only five. Ironically, it was Dad who found Mom her job at a magazine kiosk in the center of this university town, near one of the most stunning botanical gardens in the world. This beautiful historic city, and not the Dracula legend, was the Transylvania I knew as a child.

Mom loved running the kiosk, and was very good at it. Soon she was not only selling cigarettes, cigars, newspapers, and magazines, but tracking inventory and making sure that supplies were replenished so customers had access to everything they needed—no easy thing in a Communist dictatorship.

As a little girl, I would join her at the kiosk after school. A shy child who tried my best to avoid customers, I did my homework there, and shared dinner with my mother—surrounded by pages of print. Occasionally, she let me roll tobacco or fold newspapers for her.

I will never forget the day I sold my first magazine at the kiosk: The customer smiled as he approached the window and asked me if I had the weekly magazine. Mom was replenishing inventory at the moment and was not available to make the sale.

My heart raced when I realized that it was up to me to complete the transaction. As I mentioned, I was a very shy child. My present outgoing, friendly, confident personality took years to cultivate, and I certainly wasn't there yet. People scared me—especially people I didn't know. I had spent much of my childhood in isolation or around a few family members and friends, so I was easily intimidated by strangers. When he asked me for the magazine, I gulped, reached out to the pile on the shelf below me, and thrust one in his direction without a word.

He smiled again. "How old are you?"

"Eight," I answered, dropping my gaze immediately to the floor, trying not to let my discomfort be too obvious.

"You look like a very pretty and smart girl," the gentleman responded. "My name is Smutku. What is your name?"

"Ana," I whispered.

He took the magazine, paid for it, and then he reached into his coat pocket and handed me a few wrapped chocolates. "These are from Russia," he said, "and I am certain you will like them." By then, my mom had returned to the kiosk, and Smutku introduced himself to her before he went on his way.

His one kind gesture showed me what it was like to be appreciated by a total stranger. And that was the spark that changed my life. I decided at that very moment that someday I would have my own business, and that I might even run magazine like the one I'd sold him. In that single sentence, Smutku started my mental journey from shy, awkward girl to thriving entrepreneur.

He was my first advocate in the world of business, and he had no idea. From that day on, Mr. Smutku visited us once a week. I still remember his smiling face. We became friends, and he told me all about his family, his children in Russia, and how hard it was for him to work in another country, where he could not see them very often. My heart hurt for him, as I could hardly imagine what it would be like to be separated from my own parents.

Four decades later, in 2006, still remembering that chance encounter, I finally created a magazine of my own: E-Play Magazine, Inc.

The E stands for *electronic*—a representation of today's high-tech world that didn't even exist in 1958. And the word *play* stands for lightness, for recharging one's spirit through the articles in the magazine. Not only is it a personal reminder to me of that day at the kiosk when I sold my first magazine, it also reminds me that now I get to play.

I was already thinking and acting like an adult at age eight, back in Romania. To be even more precise, I don't remember having carefree, playful thoughts after about age five—except during our few weeks in the spa town of Borsec every summer from the time I was six until we left Romania. One summer, something happened there that changed my life; let me tell you the full story of how it happened.

Borsec is a delightful resort town filled with huge old pine trees, where people enjoy mineral waters for healing and recreation. This mountain town has small produce shops, cafeterias, one movie house and lots of little guest homes—and spectacular ice-filled caves.

Mom would book an inexpensive bed-and-breakfast and we would take simple pleasures together: walk in town, carry long bottles to fill with different mineral waters, visit the caves, hike, eat fresh pastries, go to the movies, and meet other visitors from all over Europe.

As the only child of a single mother, I felt that when Mom and I were together in Borsec, my world was complete—and closed to others.

But then Mom met Samuel Gluck, a high school teacher, a deeply spiritual man who loved children and loved his work. Mr. Gluck had no family at all.

I was almost eight years old when we met him. At first, I was okay with him joining us on our walks—and I certainly enjoyed the pastries he bought for us. He always tried to draw me into conversation, but I was shy and answered in monosyllables.

The following year he joined us again. By then, I wasn't too happy about it because it meant less time to hang out alone with Mom.

A couple of days before we were to return to Cluj. Mom and I were just about ready to eat our fancy lunch of fresh brown bread with butter, sliced and very fresh red peppers, tomatoes and cucumbers, and fresh-made lemonade.

Mr. Gluck knocked on our door with a huge smile on his face: "I bought 3 tickets to the soccer game and these were the last ones—so we are going to the game at 4 p.m. this afternoon."

Mom was thrilled, but I was upset that we'd miss our afternoon walk through town. We had to climb a big hill to get to the game. On our way, I faked a huge sore in my knee; "I can't go up anymore," I said. "We need to go back home and see what's wrong with my knee," and I began to limp. Of course, they took me seriously, so we walked back down to our lodge. They sat me down on the veranda chair and put my leg up on the other chair.

Yet my victory was hollow. I felt enormously guilty—and I more than 50 years later, I still feel awful about it.

Half an hour later, we suddenly heard music and bells and drums. A circus group was promoting their performance for the following week, and everyone was running outside to join them.

Without even thinking, I also jumped up and ran outside the lodge, shocking my mother.

"How quickly you healed, my dear!" she screamed as she grabbed my arm and dragged me inside. "I cannot believe what you did. How selfish of you!"

She was right, of course. Deeply ashamed, I ran, crying, into my room and closed the door.

Mr. Gluck knocked. I opened it, chastised and embarrassed. "Sorry," I said.

"You have a right to punish me—"

Mr. Gluck smiled as he cut off my long apology. "When I was a little boy, your age, my father asked me to help sweep outside our home. I told him I had a toothache and I had to go take a nap. He told me, 'Five minutes ago you bit on the biggest potato candy; I believe you're pretending to have a toothache—but instead of punishing you, I will teach you a prayer.' I'm going to do that for you."

Mr. Gluck took me outside, sat me down and shared a most beautiful Hebrew prayer, the Modeh Ani, a powerful prayer of thanksgiving that shifted my attitude from taking the day for granted to being grateful and appreciating the arrival of each new day. Religious Jews traditionally recite this prayer before they even get out of bed; I still pray it every morning. (You can see this prayer and its English translation at http://en.wikipedia.org/wiki/Modeh_Ani)

That moment changed my whole spirit. I will always be grateful to Mr. Gluck for teaching me something so meaningful and positive, shifting from punishment to a blessing when he had every right to punish me.

Sometimes I feel that I have to make it up to my younger self, cheated out of a normal childhood by hard circumstances.

But my lack of a typical childhood never buried me in anger or disappointment. Instead, I turned everything into a new opportunity and a new skill. Special moments, like being treated so kindly by Mr. Smutku and Mr. Gluck, became positive forces for success throughout my life.

CHAPTER 2

Uprooting at age ten

Takeaway Tools:

- **Take the Right Risks: Rebooting is Hard—But Worth It.** Leaving behind everyone you know and everything you've done can be traumatic. Keep the goals in sight: why you've chosen to do this, and how your life will improve.
- **Some Gifts Should be Accepted—And Some Refused.** It's important to recognize when a gift would actually reverse your progress. Even though we had no money and no place to go, refusing an inappropriate apartment in an unworkable location was the right move for us. Yet saying yes to the offer to live with my mother and her new husband was absolutely the right thing.
- **Power of Prayer.** When you open your heart to God, your prayers are heard—and sometimes answered.

Mom's dream from the day I was born was to leave Romania and move to Israel. As a Holocaust survivor, she wanted to live in a country where she felt she belonged—where she could bring up her child as openly Jewish, without fear or shame. It took ten years, but we finally obtained our very first passports and all of the necessary documentation.

And so, after months of planning and preparation, my mom and I—expecting a secure and prosperous future—finally emigrated from Romania to Israel when I was ten. I still remember the excitement that surrounded our decision to go.

In Romania, we had lived in a small apartment on the fourth floor. The elevator didn't run well, so Mom and usually I walked up and down the stairs. We shared a bathroom with two other families, and my bath nights were Tuesdays and Fridays. I loved those days—it felt so good to be scrubbed clean!

We owned nothing but a few pieces of clothing, some books, shoes, and a few knickknacks. Life in Romania was meager. Yet, my mom still found ways to illuminate the dull, gray days. She introduced me to the opera, classical music, and the ballet. I was exposed to a rich culture, but I was still a poor, sad little girl.

We packed our suitcases with our few precious belongings and imagined our promising future. My mom and I were sure that in no time, we'd live in a nice home and replenish all that we were leaving behind. We said goodbye to classmates and friends, while Mom trained her successor at the kiosk.

My heart constricted when I said goodbye to my father, not knowing when I would see him again. The finality and uncertainty was almost unbearable. My life in Cluj may not have been wonderful, but it was comfortable—and familiar. I knew what to expect.

I thought of Mr. Smutku, torn from his children, when Mom and I stepped onto the train to go to Hungary, and from there to Austria, where we could take our very first plane trip to Tel Aviv. I would miss his smile. But we were off on an exotic adventure to a promising future, and I couldn't afford to look back.

Mom and I hung all of our dreams on our move to Israel. We believed this country would give us a whole new life, a new beginning, and endless opportunities. We focused on the excitement of our future and pushed forward. As we arrived in Israel, peeling off our heavy winter clothes on a hot, sunny January day, it was as if we were shedding our skins.

Then cruel reality set in.

A charitable organization had given us keys to a small one-bedroom apartment and a modest amount of money to help us get by for the first few days. The apartment building was surrounded by an open field with no roads and hardly any people. We were city people, and Mom immediately felt anxious and fearful. What were we going to do here?

The school was twenty miles from our apartment. So were any grocery stores or outdoor market. Panic built up in our throats as we stared at the three containers of food on the kitchen floor: a can of olives, a bottle of oil, and a jar of jam. There were also a few bags of crackers and a bottle of some kind of juice.

Food was not abundant back in Romania, but we didn't go hungry. Mom and Dad made sure that I always had a meal. My stomach growled as I sought comfort in my mother's eyes. But she looked just as weak and lost as I felt.

We gazed at our new surroundings in horror.

Mom decided immediately that we could not stay there. We locked the door behind us and took the bus into the city, to her sister's address. That's when we received the second blow. To our shock, Mom's sister, with a sick husband to care for, had moved to another city, and we had no way to find her. Instead, we got on another bus—to Tel Aviv, the big city.

By the time we arrived, it was already early evening. We had no place to stay and no food. Mom and I walked to a nearby deli and collapsed into our seats. Mom ordered a bowl of soup and some bread. I was exhausted, hungry, and homeless—it was the best soup I had ever tasted!

We ended up sleeping in the police station that night, and with the help of the police, Mom tracked down her nephew—the son of her oldest brother who had been killed in the war. What a relief to find a family member! He took us into his home, and we lived there for two months.

Then I was accepted into Kibbutz Mossad—a place where poor children and orphans went to school, worked, and lived. Just like Mr. Smutku's children, I would be separated from my parents.

Mom and I took the bus there, and I carried a little suitcase with a few pieces of clothing, one book, and my wooden doll. At ten years old, I would be living on my own with a bunch of kids from other countries, and I was terrified. I didn't speak any Hebrew at the time, although I did speak Hungarian, Romanian, French, and Russian.

When we arrived, a lovely lady and a young man showed us the dorm where I would do my homework and sleep. Besides the room I would share with three other girls, the kibbutz also had a dining room, kitchen, school, library, ironing rooms, wash rooms, a chicken farm, a turkey farm, a horse barn, vegetable fields, fruit-tree groves, a big warehouse filled with eggs and other products, a social hall that was also used for prayer, and several cows wandering around the grounds.

As a city girl, I felt completely out of place there. But it was my new home, and I had to make the best of it, even if I still felt like an outsider.

I took classes four hours a day, and then I did my homework, sitting on a rock outside my dorm when the weather permitted. And I worked, too. My first job was to collect the chicken eggs and bring them to the warehouse, where they were shipped to other destinations.

At first, the chickens were loud and a little frightening, but I decided I would not be intimidated by a bunch of squawking feathers. After a couple of weeks, I started singing to them while I walked around and collected the eggs. It created a much friendlier atmosphere, so I made peace with my new job.

I missed my mom terribly. She would visit me once a week, but the rest of the days I was desperately lonely and sad. My roommates were not kind to me; the only words we exchanged had to do with chores: whose turn was it to do the laundry, take out the trash, or dust the meager furniture where we stored our precious food gifts from home? My life was quite regimented. I woke up at 6:15 a.m. every morning to the shrill and unavoidable alarm bell that rang throughout the compound—it shrieked again every night at 10, for lights out—went to work when they told me to, and attended school when they expected me in the classroom. We worked around the clock, except on Saturday, the Sabbath. That was the only day I had a little free time to read and try to make sense of it all.

After three months working at the chicken farm, I was moved to the ironing room, where I helped iron clothes for Israeli soldiers. Three months later, I was moved to the fields and spent my days picking olives and oranges.

By that time, I spoke the language, and my grades were very good. I liked my teacher, but my happiest event was the day I met Riza, my first friend in Israel, in the ironing room. She was an orphan from Russia, and she had a brother there, too.

We did our homework together, read books together, and argued about the things that mattered to us—and most of all, we cared about each other—and that bit of caring in such a regimented world went a long way. I still had my parents, even though they were far away. I never knew how she lost hers; I never asked, and she did not volunteer any information.

I felt so lucky to have Riza as a friend. Riza was blonde, and I was a brunette. Like me, she was slender and tall for her age, and an introvert. But what really cemented our friendship was sharing the hardships that we experienced before either of us turned eleven years old. Oh, how tired we felt at the end of the day! We laughed from exhaustion.

Saturday remained our very special day. After breakfast, we went to pray at the local hall. These were the first days in my life that I had an opportunity to connect with God, and I was surprised by how comforting it was to get to know my Higher Power. I shared everything that was on my mind and all the details of my new life in Israel with God. And I brought along the Modeh Ani prayer I'd learned from Mr. Gluck, back in Romania.

I didn't ask for much. Only one prayer was constant: to live with Mom again and feel like we were a family.

It was the first time I had ever asked anything of God, and to my amazement, God answered my prayers. Eleven months after I entered the kibbutz, my mother came to take me home. She had been courted by a sweet elderly widower, who was looking to remarry. Mom told him that she would only marry him if he let me move in with them, too. He had three grown kids, and he understood my mother's plea.

Mom picked me up from the dorm and took me to his elegant house in the most posh area of Tel Aviv—from rags to riches in a matter of hours. I had my own room, my own bathroom, and a balcony to go outside and do my homework, if I wanted. Mom registered me in a private school, and life changed for me overnight.

In just over a year, I'd had two deep, dramatic changes in my life. This time, I was grateful for it.

CHAPTER 3

How to make friends with money

Takeaway Tools:

- **90 Days to Change Your Patterns.** Spend three months to retrain your brain.
- **Plan Your Portions.** Learn to divide your days, weeks, and months into productive chunks to accomplish important tasks.

Every step of my life has taught me an important lesson about cash flow. The first and most important lesson I learned at a very young age was to shift my attitude: money could no longer be a source of stress; it had to become my friend.

We'll come back to my story later, but first, it's time to show you how you, too, can make money into a friend and ally—in this chapter and the two that follow it.

Attitude is everything. Once you change your attitude toward money, doors of possibility will open to you. As a small girl working alongside my mom in the kiosk in Romania, or as a student living with other poor children and orphans in Kibbutz Mossad, I never could have imagined how abundant the world really was, once I opened myself up to that abundance. It's been a great journey—and you can succeed, too.

Throughout the rest of this book, I'll show you how embracing the cash flow has created wondrous things in my life—and how you can tap into that abundance, as well. But in order to make the most use of this mindset, you need basic money skills and a framework to use them. And that's exactly what I'm going to give you in these next three chapters.

Just as these three chapters prepare you for the work we'll do together, we start the process of making friends with money with a little preparation. When you prepare, you become a master of your most valuable asset: time.

Passion, Priority, and Portion: A 3-Step/90-Day Program

Passion, Priority, and Portion—the magical three Ps that have anchored my success—are the biggest gifts I have to share with you. In the next few pages, you'll learn the easy (almost effortless) **3-Step/90-Day Program** that I created originally to develop the three Ps in my own life. In just 10 minutes a day, you'll discover and explore your passion and priorities, and use powerful **Portioning Worksheets** to efficiently distribute your activities over your available time. Because this program focuses on the NOW, it will help you find and nourish your passion seed, and guide you as you clarify your priorities.

Relax and enjoy this process! Don't worry about the outcome. Stay in the now, and you will discover the answers you seek.

The 3-Step/90-Day Program is central to implementing the Three P Formula of Passion, Priority, and Portion that we'll explore in the next chapter. It took me about eight years to develop and perfect it: first training myself, then refining it as I trained my life coaching clients.

But even though I spent eight years working on it, the 3-Step/90-Day Program requires very little of your time: just 10 minutes a day for 90 consecutive days—and you can probably find 10 minutes a day in 50 different ways. For instance, cut your "warm-up" time on your to-do list and plunge right in...slice the vegetables while the pasta water is heating, instead of waiting for the noodles to be done...knock five minutes from your morning getting-ready routine and trim three visits to the bathroom by two minutes each...

Yet this tiny bit of time can yield impressive results—especially if you block out the same 10 minutes each day—whether it's 7:12 to 7:21 every morning before you go to work, 12:47 to 12:56 in the afternoon as you're finishing your lunch hour, or any other consistent time that works for you. The program works best when your mind and body know ahead of time that those 10 minutes are already devoted to creating a friendship with money, and nothing can stand in their way.

You work each step for 30 days. In other words, you do the first 10-minute activity on days 1-30, the second activity for days 31-60, and the last activity over days 61-90. Each activity builds on what you've already done.

The power of the 3-Step/90-Day Program comes from its simplicity and ease with which you can do it. Don't you want to change your life in just 10 minutes a day?

Step 1: The First 30 Days

This is a hard one. Are you ready?

Take 10 minutes—at the same time every day for 30 days—and do ABSOLUTELY NOTHING! Don't skip this step, even if you don't believe you need it. Give it a chance!

The Benefit

It sounds counterintuitive, but the benefits of doing nothing are spectacular. When you do absolutely nothing for 10 minutes, on 30 consecutive days, you will begin to de-clutter your thoughts and rejuvenate your spirit. It will recharge your batteries with clarity and amazing new energy. And it will help you say goodbye to stress, worry, and fear.

Just as a gardener must clear the weeds to make room for the garden to grow, de-cluttering your mind will make room for your passion seed to flourish. We all have the passion seed within us, but that seed has to grow before we can really see it, feel it, and make it a part of our core. The 10 minutes of quiet nurture that passion seed; they fertilize, remove the weeds around it, and make room for your own passion to grow.

You may think doing nothing doesn't require instruction. You're right—but it does require the right mindset. Thus, here are some guidelines (not rules) that I have found help this practice to go deeper:

Sit in a comfortable chair, in a room or outdoor space with a comfortable temperature, and wear comfortable clothing.

Turn off the TV, computer, radio, music player, and any other possible source of interruption—even your phone.

Stare at a nondescript object. You can close your eyes (as long as you don't nod off).

Push aside the thoughts that stream through your mind.

After 30 days of doing nothing for 10 minutes each day, you're ready for Step 2.

Step 2: The Second 30 Days

Once again, set aside the same 10 minutes every day for each of the second 30 days. This time, write down three things you desire in your life. You can use a piece of paper, a notebook, or a computer. They can be ideas, material things, goals…whatever you choose to bring into your life that day. Ponder those three things for 10 minutes. What are your thoughts? How do you feel when you think about them? Each day, you make your list. It could be the same three things each day, or you can replace any or all of them, as long as you always have three on your list.

The Benefit

The three things you desire, write down, and then contemplate will reflect your growing passion seed. As you continue to write and think and feel, some items will fall by the wayside, replaced by others. Note which ones get pushed off the list. They are important to you, but their priority is not as great as the things that replaced them.

At the end of the 30 days, you'll know three solid desires that truly reflect your passion. Ten daily minutes of contemplation and reflection on the things you want in your life will lead you to greater enthusiasm and determination—and ultimately, greater happiness.

Step 3: The Third 30 Days

You've been cultivating these three things for 30 days—now, you're ready to bring them into your life. Take the same 10 minutes every day for each of the third 30 days to TAKE ACTION on your three goals. Make specific plans to turn them into reality. Start with broad outlines on the first day, and work toward step-by-step details as the 30 days progresses. Correct and adjust your plans, as you begin to fill in the details.

Note: You may be tempted to jump directly to Step 3. Don't! By going through the whole 3-step process and taking the whole 90 days, you will articulate your true passion seed much more deeply and clearly. And when you do move into action, that action is much more likely to create permanent positive change—because you've been warming up and training your brain, just as an Olympic athlete warms up and trains. Now your very powerful mind (and mindset) is ready to help you meet those deep inner desires.

The Benefit

At the end of the third 30 days, you'll have a workable plan to bring three things you're passionate about into your life. You'll be ready, eager, and determined to bring those plans into reality by acting on them one step at a time.

And by this time, you'll already start to see results. Time will begin to work for you, and you will be ready to portion its forward flow.

Portioning Worksheets

The way to get your action plan done is to divide your day into smaller pieces, and assign tasks or goals to each portion. I call this "portioning." Plan to portion the 1,440 minutes of each day so that some part of every day reflects your passions and priorities.

Most of us have planners to schedule our time. Yet most of us don't accomplish everything that we enter into our planners—because they don't reflect our passion and priority. Your Portioning Worksheets don't replace your planners—but they will help you think about how your activities can advance your passions and priorities, *before* you enter them in your planner. The worksheets also give you feedback by allowing you to reflect on the activities you actually perform.

In the rest of this chapter, you'll find separate worksheets for months, weeks, and days. Like all the worksheets in this book, you can photocopy them or download them from **www.themoneyflow.com/worksheets** and use them over and over. This makes it easy to generate a fresh list every day, carry over not-done items without retyping, and instantly sort by any column.

Portioning Your Month

When you portion your month, list the activities you expect to accomplish and assign a priority to each. Use any priority ranking that works for you. For me, I find a scale of 1 (highest priority) to 5 (lowest priority) works nicely. And it's perfectly fine to give more than one activity the same priority ranking.

Include both the activities you *must* do and the activities you *choose* to do. After completing the list, identify the month and year for future reference. You may find it helpful to put the completed worksheets in a binder or a computer folder, so you can not only refer back to them whenever you want, but you can chart your progress toward your goals. After a couple of years, you'll be amazed at how you've been able to embrace and achieve much larger passions.

Each Monthly Activities Worksheet is like a chapter heading in a book; the weekly sheets are subsections and the daily accomplishments logs fill out the chapter. So your binder might look something like this:

April
- Week One
  - Day One
  - Day Two
  - Day Three
  - Day Four
  - Day Five
  - Day Six
  - Day Seven
- Week Two
  - Day One
  - Day Two
  - Day Three
  - Day Four
  - Day Five
  - Day Six
  - Day Seven
- Week Three
  - Day One
  - Day Two

Day Three
Day Four
Day Five
Day Six
Day Seven
Week Four
Day One
Day Two
Day Three
Day Four
Day Five
Day Six
Day Seven

May
Week One
Day One
Day Two
Day Three
Day Four
Day Five
Day Six
Day Seven
Week Two
Day One
Day Two
Day Three
Day Four
Day Five
Day Six
Day Seven
Week Three
Day One
Day Two
Day Three
Day Four
Day Five
Day Six
Day Seven
Week Four
Day One
Day Two
Day Three

Day Four
Day Five
Day Six
Day Seven

Use your Monthly Activities Worksheet to fill in entries in your planner. This worksheet gives you the big picture. It allows you to think about *what*, instead of just *when*—and that lets you find time to work on tasks that are important—maybe even crucial—but not urgent. If you only use a planner, and therefore focus only on the *when*, you could far too easily get bogged down in the things that seem urgent but aren't all that important, and you could neglect to make time for the important things. This system makes sure the important steps you need to achieve your deepest goals are not left off.

You can even include activities for the next month, but be clear that they don't have priority for the current month. I assign a priority of 0 to future activities.

Here's a sample Monthly Activities Worksheet:

Monthly Activities			
Want To Do		Priority	
Need To Do			
Month/Year			

Portioning Each Week

Now, portion your weeks: write the beginning date on the sheet, list the activities you want to accomplish, and *assign a day and length of time you'll work on it to each activity*. So you don't get overwhelmed, only include the activities you intend to do this week, even if you still have other to-do items on your Monthly Activities Worksheet. Now, transfer these tasks to your planner. This ensures that you make time to accomplish your most important priorities. Here's a sample Weekly Activities Worksheet:

Weekly Activities	Day(s)
Beginning Date for Week	

Portioning Your Days

Portioning your months and weeks is a looking-ahead activity. But when you portion your days, you have to look back. Your Daily Activities Worksheet lets you fine-tune your planning based on what you actually got done. Unlike the Monthly and Weekly worksheets, you don't use it to fill in your planner or calendar. Instead, you check in to see how well your plan is working.

Date the sheet and list each activity you performed during the day along with notes about whether you had allocated the right amount of time, or too much/too little, and whether the task was effective.

Here's a sample Daily Activities Worksheet:

Daily Activities	Timing / Effectiveness
Day/Date	

Congratulations—by completing the 3-Step/90-Day Program and the Portioning Worksheets, you're already preparing to make friends with money and to experience positive cash flow. You're cultivating fertile ground to nurture and grow your passion seed—and making space in your life to work on turning your deepest hopes and desires into reality.

That preparation will be crucial as we move forward, in the next chapter—and learn more about the three Ps: passion, priority, and portion.

CHAPTER 4

Staying friends with money, for life

Takeaway Tools:

- **Use the 3 Ps.** Create a positive relationship with money.
- **Create Better Habits.** It doesn't happen by itself, and it takes time.

Let me ask you a question:

Why are you unhappy?

Is it because…

You didn't get what you wanted?

Things went wrong?

Someone disappointed you?

Can you relate to any of those responses?

If you think you're unhappy because of "reasons" like these, you're wrong.

Everyone faces challenges that could lead to feeling unhappy—but not everybody chooses to be unhappy!

Actually, this is the wrong question to ask in the first place. If you find an answer to the question—if all you do is figure out and fix the problems that let you justify being unhappy—you still won't be happy. You might even be *more* unhappy, because your excuses are gone.

Let's put a positive spin on this question instead:

What will make you happy?

This is the real question! When you understand what will make you happy and then do it, you will be happy no matter how many "reasons"—or excuses—you might have to be unhappy.

So why all the questions about happiness?

Happiness is very closely related to your relationship with money—not money itself, but your relationship with it. As you establish and build your positive friendship with money, you must realize that money by itself cannot make you happy, no matter how much you have. The real power is in your *relationship* with money.

To stay friends with money, we have to build a relationship with it—a healthy relationship. We all spend time building relationships with family members, friends, coworkers, neighbors, children, and spouses—yet most of us never even consider spending a little time cultivating a relationship with money. Here's how to pursue and nourish a relationship with money that will last a lifetime, in just three words—"the three Ps":

- Passion
- Priority
- Portion

As I mentioned earlier, the three Ps have been instrumental in my long friendship with money.

What do these three words have to do with cash flow? For me, they've been the source of an abundant financial life.

Passion

Passion is powerful. It changes your motivation from merely avoiding negative consequences to embracing the joy, energy, and excitement of the things that put zing in your life. Passion ignites your spirit and makes your life feel fulfilled. Life without passion is dull and meaningless—but with passion, you have no limits!

Passion gives you the extra energy you need to overcome any of the challenges you face. It leads directly to a happy, content, and unique life. It's the seed that will feed your soul, and when it blossoms, you will truly know what it is to live in a positive mindset.

So how do you find your passion? Sometimes it may be hard to identify, because it's not the same in every person. But I have some really good news for you: all you have to do is get in touch with your thoughts and feelings to uncover that passion seed. When you find it, give it prominence in your life—and watch it grow.

Here are some questions to help you identify your passion seed:

What is important to me?

What do I really enjoy doing?

What am I good at?

Which of the following spark my interest (these are examples; feel free to use your own)?

Working with children
Sports
Learning and reading
Arts, painting, music, theatre
Working with numbers
Writing
Public speaking
Designing homes, architecture
Research
Medicine and cures
Travel
Politics and current events
Investing money
Helping others

When you identify your life passion, turn your energy toward it. As you zero in on your passion and give it the time it deserves, the cash flow will follow.

People always tell me that they wish they could bottle up my energy. I almost always have a big smile on my face and a sparkle just underneath the surface. And that zing of energy comes directly from passion. Not only did I find my passion, I nurture and cherish it every day—and so can you.

What's your passion? Are you giving it the attention it deserves?

Priority

Once you begin to nourish your passion seed, you'll become very strongly motivated to do only those things that you feel passionate about. But here in the real world, you also have to make time for your other obligations. Thus, developing a healthy sense of Priority is the next step in organizing your life and opening up to a positive cash flow.

There are 1,440 minutes in a day—but unless you prioritize, they slip away so quickly! Priority allows you to balance the things you're eager to do with the things you need to do.

Let's look a bit deeper: Priority is the sense that one thing is more important than another..So ultimately, priority means understanding the relative importance of various activities, and shifting time to accomplish the most important ones.

Three simple considerations can help you determine priorities:

1. **Common Sense.** You develop common sense through your life experiences, more than from books or classes. You learn what works and what doesn't work in the real world, and you fine-tune your future actions accordingly.
2. **Outside Demands.** What others require from you. These things are out of your control, but you must consider them if you plan to maintain healthy business and personal

relationships. You are not an island—so factor in the needs and desires of those around you.

3. **Timing.** Everything has its time. As you mature, you'll discover that timing is essential to accomplishing your priorities. Timing develops as you gain experience and wisdom. With practice, you'll learn how much time and attention to give certain matters—and when to focus your attention in a different direction.

As demands pile up in your life, using these three factors to prioritize will help you complete tasks more easily and with a lot less stress. Priority also allows you to stay in the now. You can concentrate on your priority activity, because you recognize that it needs your attention first.

When you can stay "in the now" with an activity, you'll accomplish it faster and more easily than if you constantly have to grapple with what you need to do next. Priority gives you focus. It shows you how to become more efficient and frees up time to further pursue your passion.

Portion

Portion is a part of a whole. It's also a very useful tool to distribute your prioritized activities over those 1,440 minutes in the day.

You become even more adept at portioning when you learn to *apportion.*

What does that mean? Apportion means to distribute according to a plan or for a special purpose. Note that phrase, *according to a plan*. It's not random. Planning will allow you to allocate time portions according to each activity's priority and the actual amount of time the task takes to complete.

Let's talk about three kinds of activities:

1. Casual
2. Planned
3. Unplanned

We perform casual activities as opportunities come along, and they don't interfere with higher priorities. For instance, you remember as you're driving by the grocery store that you're out of milk. Stopping to buy it will only take an extra five minutes, and you can cross the task off your list. It's more efficient than going home and then back out again to make a special trip to the store.

For planned activities, you block out the right portion of time to conduct the activity. You plan for it; you put it on the schedule. So, if a client proposal is due tomorrow and it will take you an hour to write it, you schedule a specific hour on today's calendar to write the proposal. When you get to that hour, the proposal is your priority.

Unplanned activities pop up suddenly and become your highest priority; they grab time portions you'd committed to other activities. As an example, a medical emergency immediately becomes your top priority and reserves whatever portion of your time you need until it can be resolved.

Always divide your day into smaller portions; you'll complete many more activities when you divide your day into one-or two-hour portions than if you try to wrap your mind around what to do for 1,440 minutes.

Because things don't always go according to plan, you can create additional time portions by adding casual activities to planned activities—also known as multitasking. The better you get at portioning your time, the more extra minutes you'll have to pursue your passion.

You'll discover numerous ways to portion your time. You can become a master of arranging these chunks of minutes to create room to breathe—and enjoy life as you pursue your proper balance and flow.

When a shipment of cars arrives in an American port, all of the cars don't get sent to one location. They're divided up according to demand and shipped to many destinations across the United States.

In the same way, when you portion out your time, you divide the total number of minutes into smaller portions, and harness them throughout the day. Portion is vital both to sustain your personal life and to honor your business commitments.

As tools to help you take control of your life, these three Ps help you create balance. You will neither be a slave to money nor feel as though you have to enslave it. That's not the kind of relationship you're looking for. Instead, you're developing a relationship that makes you understand and respect the importance of money and its role in the course of your life.

As you get in touch with your Passion, Priorities, and Portion, you'll easily develop a creative relationship with money that initiates a positive flow throughout everything you do. It becomes a simple giving and receiving motion—when, why, where, and what portion of your money to spend or save. That's the dance.

Perfecting this dance and filtering your relationship through a positive overall attitude will create a successful relationship with money—without intimidation, fear, judgment, or anger. You'll drop all the bad habits from your former relationship with money and pursue a much stronger partnership.

CHAPTER 5

Why money must circulate

Takeaway Tools:

- **Money has to Flow.** Keeping it bottled up makes money your unwilling slave, not your friend and companion.
- **When Money Does Flow, it "Floats All Boats."** The whole economy revolves around money circulating from one person or business to another, to another.

Now, let's look at another question:

Why must money circulate? Why can't we just keep all the money we collect for ourselves and hide it away under mattresses and bury it in jars in the backyard?

Good question!

Money must circulate, because that is the only way we truly develop a relationship with it. When we circulate money, we become the masters of that relationship, as we build it each and every day.

This cycle is also crucial for our global economy. For example, when you decide to take a vacation to recharge and rejuvenate your life, you buy airline tickets, pay for accommodations, buy meals, and purchase gifts during your stay. You boost local economies in the places you visit, and you help travel businesses build their successes, as well. When money circulates, everyone benefits.

Unhealthy relationships with money breed fear and insecurity, which often cause people to stop circulating money.

But that's dangerous, because it halts the give-and-take that allows all of us to thrive. Don't hold too tightly to money. When the circulatory system in our bodies shuts down or is damaged, we get sick—and the same principle applies to money. When you stop its circulation, the entire system becomes constipated. Holding on to money has never helped anyone succeed. Cash*flow* is the key to success, not cashstashing.

Of course, I'm not suggesting that you run out and spend all your money in order to be successful. Excess is equally unhealthy. Moderation is key. Over the years, I've learned that there's a delicate balance here. I had to find out the hard way how important it is to both stay within my means and also overcome my fear of not having enough money. I had to stop constantly craving more and decide that I was quite satisfied with what I had. In the next chapters, you'll see how I reached that delicate balance. It wasn't an easy process, but I am so grateful that I learned this in time to create a healthy relationship with money.

In the last few chapters, you discovered how you can make money your friend. Now that you have a new outlook on money, you'll start to enjoy the ease it can represent and the things you can acquire with it.

And you'll also learn to make adjustments when you have less of it. Sometimes you have to work harder for your money or make other proactive plans to maintain a healthy relationship with your new friend.

When money circulates, trust and maturity come into the relationship. Just as when your kids leave for college, you still love them and think about them and wish them the best—but you no longer see them daily. You might get an occasional text, email, or phone call, but you have to trust that they are doing the right things and leading productive, happy, healthy lives.

The same holds true when you let money circulate. You may decide to invest it somewhere, and for a while, your cash flow is lower.

But you trust that you've maintained a healthy relationship with money, and the end results will ultimately be fruitful. Money is your friend for life. It will eventually flow back to you if you continue to cultivate a positive relationship with it.

In Part 2, I'll take you through my own evolving journey to a positive friendship with money, using the lens of my own very diverse career. Together, we'll look at every job I've had, and you'll see how my attitude through triumphs and setbacks helped me learn to make friends with money—and stay friends for life. I'll tell the story of that job, and we'll look at the lessons it taught me, and how you can apply them in your own life. Yes, your life path will be different. But the lessons of my life will find parallels in yours.

Remember: like any healthy relationship, positive cash flow starts with a positive attitude. Because I desire a great relationship with money, I spend time cultivating it. Money helps me fulfill my dreams; it's become a great friend and ally. You, too, will become friends with money, if you take these tips and lessons to heart.

I'm excited that we get to share this journey together. Ready to get started?

PART II

The Ladder of Success: Money Lessons from Every Job

Success is a ladder—and I've taken more steps up that ladder in every single job I've had. From unpaid assistant to my mother selling magazines in the kiosk in Romania to managing multi-million dollar companies in the United States, I've extracted gems—lessons in success—every time.

I took one company from annual revenues of $250,000 to $62 million in five years. I helped another organization climb from $100,000 to $12 million in just three years. In my current position, despite a crippling recession, I've tripled sales to reach $30 million.

These achievements did not happen by accident. They're the result of thousands of money flow lessons I've learned along the way.

In the next chapters, I'll share the secrets of success that I learned from every position I've ever held. Because I continue to apply these lessons, the ladder of my success weaves its way toward the stratosphere. You'll see how to apply these lessons to your own business and career, and build your own ladder of success.

CHAPTER 6

The Ogress: Learning from my first and worst boss

Takeaway Tools:

- **Kindness.** Even when people are difficult, have empathy for them. In many cases, you'll make a better human being out of your former enemy—and this will make your own situation better. Even if the other person doesn't change, others will notice and appreciate your attitude.
- **Persistence.** Don't give up too easily! Hardships test us and make us stronger. Stay with the challenge and show it your strength; when you succeed in tough circumstances, it feels even better.

Almost eighteen, I'd just graduated high school in Israel when I landed my very first job—working at a company exporting various tools to Europe and Australia.

My office was on the second floor of the company's three-story building; my title was "Assistant to Mrs. Schechter, International Documentation Manager." I fell in love with my small office and its tiny desk, telephone, and leather chair the moment Mrs. Schechter walked me there on a gloomy Thursday morning.

Mrs. Schechter's office ashtray on her desk was already filling up when I arrived at 8:30 that morning. I wondered what time she started working, but I didn't bother to ask. I felt happy and proud to land this job.

However, Mrs. Schechter seemed terribly intimidating. An elderly woman with no partners or children, she wasn't warm. She brusquely and completely buried my desk beneath a huge pile of papers. Insisting that the entire pile had to be completed within two weeks, she showed me an instruction manual.

"You will figure it out. Just follow the manual, and please try not to disturb me with questions. Consolidate them and ask me once in three days," she barked over her shoulder as she closed the door behind her.

A rush of competing emotions came over me. I wanted to work and learn, but I surely wasn't going to get help or support from Mrs. Schechter! I would either have to make it work on my own or walk out and try to get another job elsewhere.

I decided to stay. I began reading the instruction manual and organizing all the loose papers piled up on my desk by sender and subject.

When I finally took my lunch hour that very first day, two other employees approached me as I headed toward the company cafeteria.

"Are you Mrs. Schechter's new assistant?"

"Yes," I smiled.

With concerned expressions, they replied, "We hope you will last longer than the others! No one can work with her or for her; she is simply impossible, and the only reason they keep her in the company is because she is a good workhorse, very knowledgeable, and this job is her life. She works from 6 a.m. to 7 p.m. every day, and she even takes work home with her."

"Thank you for the warning," I answered, "but I will try to be an exception."

We ended up in different food lines. I had to finish in thirty minutes, according to Mrs. Schechter's orders.

After five difficult and stressful weeks, I made a breakthrough.

Sunday morning beginning my sixth week, I noticed Mrs. Schechter was coughing and pale, with dark circles around her eyes. I got up my courage and asked her if she wanted me to get her some homemade chicken soup from the deli nearby.

Pleased and shocked, she answered, "Yes, that would be nice. But why would you do such a thing for me? After all, I treat you with no human gentleness or friendliness."

Taken aback, I didn't know what to say at first. I even surprised myself when I quietly replied, "True, I am not feeling at home here. But at the end of the day, we are all people. If we can be of help to one another, why not?" I felt sorry for this lonely and bitter woman.

Mrs. Schechter handed me some money, and I got her a bowl of soup with some French bread.

That afternoon she gained a bit of color in her face and was coughing a little less after her "Jewish penicillin." And although we didn't speak that afternoon, the energy shifted permanently; I felt much more at home.

The next few days went by quickly. Mrs. Schechter began using a softer voice and even complimented me on my work—something I'd never expected. And I learned that even an ogress can soften under the pressure of kindness.

That Friday morning, Mrs. Schechter asked me to go to the bank and drop off some documents. I was happy to get out of the office and briskly walked the few blocks from our office.

The Foreign Currency Department manager at the bank asked me to sit down after I dropped off the documents. To my amazement, she smiled widely and said, "We heard about you and your success working with Mrs. Schechter. You must be different from all the others working with her. We would love to hire you to work for me here at the bank. We will pay for your lunch. We will also pay for you to go to school and adjust the hours to your academic schedule."

Was I dreaming? No! It was a real offer. I was overwhelmed. Finally, I answered, "Thank you so much for your kind offer, but I must talk to Mrs. Schechter and help her hire someone else to take my position."

The manager was even more impressed with my response.

When I returned to my office and told Mrs. Schechter, she was angry and upset at first.

"They are stealing you away from me," she shouted. But a few minutes later, she calmed down and looked at me straight in the eyes. "You, young girl, deserve this opportunity, and I wish you the best of luck. I am glad that you will stay here until I find a replacement, and I promise you one thing: I need to change if I don't want to work alone for the rest of my life. You taught me a good lesson, Ana; you restored my faith in people all over again. It's been gone too long, dear child."

I just smiled.

It took four weeks to find and train a replacement. By then, I'd developed a few simple techniques to deal with the deadlines, and the young man taking over seemed happy and at ease working with Mrs. Schechter. I walked away with a sunny feeling in my heart and accepted the position at the bank.

Once in a while, I would visit Mrs. Schechter; to everyone's surprise, we became friends. The young gentleman stayed there for years, until Mrs. Schechter retired. When she died five years after her retirement, I even felt a certain compassion for her.

To this day, like a first love, I still cherish the experience of working with her and the lessons I learned from my very brief first job.

CHAPTER 7

Shipping money around the world

Takeaway Tools:

- **Currency.** The ebb and flow of local and foreign currency, with its shifting rates of exchange, has a big impact on the global economy, and on all the little economies that are part of it.
- **Urgency.** Timing is crucial. At the bank, we always faced an urgent need to locate freight shipping company employees around the world and accurately transfer currency to pay them on time.
- **The Extra Mile.** Whenever you have a chance, go the extra mile. When I took a little extra time to help ease the minds of family members waiting back home, it made a huge difference in their lives. Just a little extra work on my part had a significant impact on them.

I joined the Maritime Bank of Israel on a Tuesday morning, promptly at 8:00 a.m.

Through my work at the bank, I developed a powerful and successful relationship with money. As I converted back and forth among 21 foreign currencies (without a computer, back then), I learned the priceless knowledge that I could work with large sums, and that my accuracy and skill made a real difference in other people's lives.

My original task was to assist Rachel, the general foreign currency manager, transferring payroll funds in the respective currencies to crew members working on Zim Shipping Freight Liners around the world. Zim transported a tremendous range of products: from clothing, canned goods and housewares, all the way to construction materials, steel, and rubber—even books and cigars.

The most important detail was to double-check the currency conversion and to make sure that it did not exceed the total amount budgeted for crew payroll. It was also extremely important that the funds were transferred on time, on the day the commitment was made by Zim. Twice a month, I had to calculate each worker's pay in his or her own currency, based on an individualized hourly rate depending on the pay scale and job title.

Zim's crew members came from all around the world. We had crews from Greece, Turkey, Italy, France, England, Portugal, Spain, Brazil, Argentina, Sweden, Norway, Finland, Holland, Japan, Germany, Romania, Yugoslavia, Bulgaria, Russia, Hungary, Poland, Australia, and the United States. The paychecks were disbursed out of several main general accounts in the United States, converted into the crew's home currency, and then distributed as part of the total payroll for that country. When one country's account was low, we had to transfer from other accounts with surplus funds. The key was to keep an average balance in each account for emergencies and disburse only according to the payroll figures for the pay period.

At first, I was uneasy in my new job. Such a huge responsibility! But after a two-week orientation and training, I made friends with the challenge and went with the flow. I concentrated on remembering that I was helping thousands of people around the world get their paychecks. This substantial income would help their families, and most importantly, the women and children back home.

Nearly all the sailors were men; I only ran across three female names among the hundreds of crew members. And their jobs were hard. They were on the water for weeks at a time, dealing with the powerful oceans and storms and weather delays, rushing to load goods, and then taking off across the rough seas to another destination.

My supervisor, Rachel, was a delightful person, always happy to share the ins and outs of this complex business; I learned so much from her. Her husband had worked for Zim before he moved on to become an Air Force pilot. Regardless of pressing deadlines and piles of work, Rachel was always pleasant and friendly. I learned from her that a pile of work is no excuse to be a pain to work with!

Every week, she'd check in about how I was coping with the flood of new things to learn, whether I liked the job and found it stimulating. I always answered with a big yes. I loved it all.

Indeed, I embraced the responsibility, and by the end of six months, I received a raise. Since the bank had promised me free tuition, I also took evening classes in business and international trade at a university. Through both my job and my courses, I was increasing my own marketability in the business world.

The bank had twenty-six employees from all corners of the world: Bulgaria, Russia, Morocco, South Africa, France, Romania, Poland, and Israel. At 18, I felt so worldly as part of this international team.

A girl from Bulgaria, a gentleman from Morocco, and I became close friends.

We went out to lunch together, talked about movies and books, and exchanged recipes. We all loved to cook, and we enjoyed comparing our different traditions and cultures. It was especially interesting talking about our childhoods and the challenges we faced as kids.

The bank was located on a busy downtown street in Tel Aviv, close to the bus station, restaurants, shops, and walking distance from the same outdoor marketplace where Mom and I had picked up food when we'd arrived homeless and penniless seven years earlier. When I visited the open market once or twice a week on my lunch hour, purchasing fresh fruits and vegetables to take home after work on the days when I had no classes, I never forgot to be grateful for how far I'd come.

This was a very good time for me professionally and personally. I loved the work I was doing, the way I was treated, the people I worked with, and the beginnings of my life as an independent adult. And I was making enough money that before long, I moved out of my stepfather's house and into a condo of my own.

The job became even more interesting when, about a year after I started working there, I was introduced, by mutual friends, to a lovely couple from Russia and Poland. The husband had been working on one of Zim's ships for several years, traveling the waters of the world. They had a little girl and a newborn baby boy. We became almost instant friends.

The woman, whose name was Klara, sewed bathing suits for GOTTEX, now a very successful swimwear company but at that time based in a garage. She was ecstatic to know I worked for the bank that paid her husband, especially once she found out that I had access to information about his ship—where he was docked, where he would sail next, etc. Imagine, in the days before cell phones and Internet, the stress of having your husband gone for three or four weeks at a time! When she didn't hear from him, her mind raced with worry. I could help ease her stress.

So, every now and then, I would inform Klara about her husband's whereabouts. When word got out about what I was doing, I began to receive phone calls from other women, and I eased their worry by providing solid, accurate information.

Rachel, my boss, realized that I was going the extra mile for people. But she was also amazed by my efficiency and how much work I produced in less than forty hours a week. Instead of being reprimanded for adding to my workload by helping these women, I was rewarded.

I received raises every six months, and I became very savvy about saving money. My first major money success was paying off the mortgage on my condo at age twenty-one.

Working for the bank, I came to understand the value of saving money. I bought almost no luxury items. Still, I was a happy young girl, and I felt I lacked nothing. With that attitude, I built a respectful relationship with money. I didn't abuse it, and it helped me live a successful, independent life.

I left my position at the bank two weeks before I gave birth to my only child,

Sean. It was hard to leave a job I so enjoyed, but I decided to stay home with my baby and give him all my motherly love—and the money I'd put aside in my years at the bank made it possible for me to do that.

On my last day, the staff at the bank gave me a huge party and lots of gifts for my baby. The ties we'd built were strong, and their outpouring of generous gifts touched my heart and helped me to confidently move into my new role as a mother.

CHAPTER 8

Stealing South America

Takeaway Tools:

- **Details.** Attention to detail is what separates a good employee from a great employee. I honed my skills in this area and prepared documentation that would pass government scrutiny.
- **Follow-up.** It's so easy for items to fall through the cracks in a business. Follow-up is key. I prepared estimated arrival times and followed up on all shipments, so that my company never lost precious inventory. This was no small task in the pre-Internet era!

The title of this chapter may be a bit deceiving, but you'll catch on soon. It begins, not in South America, but in New York City. You know what they say, "If you can make it in the Big Apple, you'll make it anywhere!"

The decision to uproot our family once again and move to another foreign land did not come lightly, but was the result of extreme circumstances. In October, 1973, seven months prior to our arrival in the United States, I was holding tightly to my son in a bomb shelter in Israel, waiting for the war to end. We lived in total blackout conditions. I found it intolerable to spend terrifying days in this kind of literal and emotional darkness, not knowing what would happen in the next moment.

On the last day of the Yom Kippur War, I made a decision to sell everything we owned—our paid-off condo, our car, and all of our belongings.

We arrived in New York City on May 5, 1974—my mother, my husband, my three-year-old son, and me. I was a young woman filled with big dreams and hopes for the future. Most importantly, I longed to taste freedom. I had heard of the spaciousness of the United States—and the incredible job and educational opportunities—and I could not wait to experience it all for myself.

We took a direct flight from Tel Aviv to New York on that very special day in May, 1974, leaving one life behind and taking a shaky step into a new world. We landed at JFK Airport with our visitors' visas, six suitcases, a few books and toys for my son, and a truckload of goals and visions for a successful, happy life in a country where we would no longer have to experience blackouts or the sounds of missiles and fighter jets zooming over our heads.

I don't know exactly what kind of reception I expected, but our arrival was not exactly triumphant. In Israel, we'd left balmy 85-degrees weather. But we stepped off the plane in New York City to a gloomy sky and a chilly 55 degrees. We all shivered as we gathered our suitcases and looked for my cousin's husband, who would be picking us up.

Even 38 years later, images from that day are still burned into my mind. I can clearly see the face of my cousin Eva's husband, Louis, as he loaded us and our few belongings into his station wagon. He was such an amazing man, well-educated and very wise. He was a beacon, a very important family connection, who helped us so much in our first days in the United States.

But I also remember the taut, worried faces of my mother, husband, and young son Sean, who began to cry as soon as we got off the plane. "Where are we going, Mommy? WHY is everything so gray outside? I don't like those big, brown buildings," he asked between his tears. "I want to go home."

For a brief moment I, too, felt a little homesick. Watching the string of ugly, brown apartment buildings fly past the window as we rode along in Louis's station wagon, I didn't feel our new country was very welcoming.

As we arrived at our cousin's home and settled in after the exhausting journey, I didn't sleep that first night. Did we make a big mistake in coming to the United States? We'd left so much behind: our familiar neighborhood, the grocery store down the street, our friends and family, my job—never again would we be a part of those communities. My heart hurt when I thought of Sean's joy riding his bike with his friends and playing in the yard back home. All of that was gone in just a few hours.

I remembered how hard it had been for my mother and me when we'd left Romania for our first land of opportunity, Israel. Sean was even younger than I had been. What had I done?

Once again, we'd decided to say goodbye to the old and embrace the new with the dream that everything would be easier in the United States. This country would give us abundance, happiness, and freedom from fear. I had to hold on to that hope.

But as in Israel, our arrival in the United States didn't start out auspiciously. And to make things even more stressful, I was the only one of the four of us who spoke English. Plus, between the stress and the drastic climate change, the other three were all sick for over a week. Yet I maintained my strength, fueled by the thought of our bright, sunny future. Nothing could dampen my high spirits.

My husband tried several jobs, but none of them worked out. We quickly burned through most of the cash we'd saved from selling everything we owned in Israel.

Still, it didn't take me long to achieve my first small victory: Five days after our arrival, I started looking for work. I scanned the newspaper ads, booked a few interviews, and marched off—armed with a great resume and a powerful letter of recommendation. I went to my first interview, and to my amazement, they hired me on the spot. It certainly helped that I spoke the language! I started working on Cedar Street, across from the World Trade Center, one week after our arrival. It was a miracle.

Now that I had a job, we settled into a modest two-bedroom apartment above a flower shop on 13th Avenue and 49th Street in the Orthodox Jewish neighborhood of Borough Park, Brooklyn. The apartment didn't look at all like our beautiful, spacious condominium back home, but nevertheless, we were happy to find our own place after spending five days imposing on our cousins.

But I was the sole breadwinner of our family, and we still couldn't make ends meet. We had to continually dip into our savings to pay the bills each month, and we had to buy a car, pay the rent, and obtain a few pieces of furniture to furnish the apartment. Since we had no local credit, we had to pay several months' rent in advance. The situation got so bad that I was forced to sell my two-carat diamond ring. We simply weren't prepared for the numerous expenses immigrants face when starting over in a foreign country.

I worked from 8:30 to 6:00 and got home by 7:00 p.m. every night. I enjoyed taking the B train from Brooklyn to the Manhattan financial district—the "money juggling place," as I used to call it.

But Sean was not very happy that I was gone such long hours. He attended half-day kindergarten at a private school, where he learned English and was also allowed to speak Hebrew, his native language. My mom picked him up at 3:00 p.m. every day, but Sean wanted to wait for me to eat dinner. From 3:00 p.m. to 7:00 p.m. every day, he watched TV, played a little, and cried a little, as he waited for my return.

Our schedule wasn't perfect, but I was so relieved to have a job. Every day, I would walk over to a nearby Chock Full o' Nuts coffee shop and buy a bowl of clam chowder and a big slice of lemon meringue pie for $1.75. After lunch, I would slowly walk back to my office, passing hundreds of people from all walks of life—all rushing somewhere in the crisp New York air.

I would take the elevator to the 23rd floor and go straight to the bathroom, where I'd cry for a few minutes. It was my daily chance to relieve the enormous stress, anxiety, and fear that came with this big life change.

A year went by, and we were down to $1,000 in our bank account, no diamond ring on my finger, but a 1970 Volvo that was paid in full, a few pieces of furniture, linen, a television set, pots and pans, and a few books in English. We were barely scraping by.

Life wasn't easy in New York. I'd planned to go to school to study the local accounting rules, but I had too much on my plate at work, and the long commute took up most of my free time.

Still, I was deeply grateful for my job. I was an assistant in document control, and my previous experience working for Mrs. Schechter and then the bank helped me tremendously. I picked up the skills I needed for this new job very quickly. By the second month, I was producing lots of work, accurately and on time.

The company I worked for exported steel tools to South America, primarily to Brazil, for construction companies, oil companies, and other big projects. The export documents had to be accurate, and most importantly, the bills of lading and the original invoices, along with copies and packing lists, had to be signed, stamped, and checked for quantity, description, purchase order number, value of goods, and the vessel transporting the goods. There were a lot of details!

I loved doing this work. The entire staff at Debra Incorporated was great. Once again, I was delighted to be surrounded by an international group of coworkers. We had people from Venezuela, Argentina, Brazil, Mexico, Puerto Rico, China, Japan, Korea, and the United States. Once a month, we'd have a potluck lunch at the office. Each of us would bring a dish from our home country, so it was quite a smorgasbord. Everyone loved my Hungarian goulash, paprikash, and blintzes, and I became more familiar with Chinese food, big steaks, and enchiladas. We had fun.

My weekly take-home pay at Debra Incorporated was $149.50, and that was considered good pay for a young woman. I had a job in Manhattan, and I felt accomplished. Yet, I was uneasy, because my paycheck didn't cover expenses. Our rent was $200 a month, and my son's school was $125 a month. Food and gas were not terribly expensive, but with all the other expenses, our cash flow was negative. Each and every month, I had to dip into our dwindling savings. Soon, there would be no money left in our bank account.

My husband had invested in a few business endeavors, but all of them failed—some because he had the wrong partners; and others because the business itself was not strong, and he hadn't properly researched the organization and its marketing plan ahead of time.

We were young and inexperienced and totally absorbed in our personal emotional adjustments. We had neglected to do our financial homework. All we knew was that we couldn't continue on the same path—so we decided to make another major change.

We packed everything we owned into our car and headed for Southern California, where sunshine and a few good friends from back home waited for us. They assured us that it would be easy for my husband to find a job in California, and he could also go to school to learn English. There was no need to deal with the harsh East Coast winters.

We were starting over—again—and this time we had even less money and a car filled with pillows, blankets, our TV set, a few personal belongings, and cooked meals for eight days on the road.

What I learned from my New York work experience was that it was hard for a family of four to survive on one small paycheck. I also learned that our living expenses could not exceed our income every month. It was a hard lesson, but I never repeated it. It taught me the importance of cash flow and money management and how to stretch my money so it would last longer.

I was one step closer to understanding cash flow.

CHAPTER 9

California clothing dreaming

Takeaway Tools:

- **Balance.** Balance what you really want to do with what you can do at the moment. I took the job in the nursing home not because I wanted to work there, but because they were hiring and I was desperate. Still, it was a chance to help others, and a powerful learning experience. So even when circumstances are not great, remember that everything will turn out just fine in the end.
- **Generosity.** If you're down and out and people offer you gifts, accept their generosity. It may be God's way of answering your prayers. Like my mother's second husband in Israel, my new boss in L.A. helped me make a fresh start when I was in need.
- **Clothing.** Clothing and fabrics have a lot to teach us. Their quality, style, and variety make an impression—good and bad. And even if you don't have money, there are ways of dressing very elegantly but also inexpensively. My sense of fashion pulled me toward success at this company.
- **Productivity AND Quality.** You don't have to choose between these virtues. Enhancing both at once will lead to a happier life and a more successful business. No need to crowd out one in favor of the other.

Good weather and the chance to live next door to old friends from Israel had lured us to Los Angeles. But we had hardly any cash left. We were BROKE. I had been the only member of the family working, and all of our funds had been depleted in

New York. I'd even had to sell my beloved diamond ring in order to purchase the old Volvo, now crammed with personal belongings, a cooler full of food, a TV set, blankets, towels, and a few toys for my four-and-a-half-year-old son.

We drove for ten days, fascinated by the vastness and variety of people, towns, and cultures across the United States—so many different expressions on different faces, such varied architecture and scenery, visiting many cities on famous Route 66 (since replaced in many spots by superhighways). By the time we arrived in California, we were exhausted. We had $600 left in our pockets. Thank God, our friends had a two-bedroom apartment ready for us to move in.

The kitchen had a refrigerator, and our friends gave us a dining room set they'd picked up at a garage sale the week before. Since we had no other furniture or money, for the first five months in California we slept on a few blankets placed on the carpet.

Life was different then. The first day after our arrival, I went with my girlfriend to the supermarket, and we filled up our carts with items to feed my family of four for an entire week—for $32.00.

As I unpacked the groceries, a huge wave of anxiety hit me: I had $568.00 left. What were we going to do? I was twenty-four, but I felt sixty-four. All night, I tossed and turned with worry. But when I woke up in the morning, I knew what I had to do.

On our way back home from the supermarket, I'd spotted a convalescent center on our corner. I got up that morning, showered, put on my navy blue trouser suit with a white-and-blue flowered top, navy shoes, and the navy purse I'd purchased in Israel.

At 7:00 a.m., I knocked on the glass window in the lobby of the convalescent center, asking for a job—any job. I told the somber older woman who answered that I was a college graduate with experience in finance and banking, but I would do any kind of work they needed.

I was hired on the spot as a nursing and personal care assistant, helping the nurses, giving medication, helping patients eat, bathe, and take walks. It wasn't the job of my dreams, but it was a job, and I was deeply grateful.

Although my shift was 6:30 a.m. to 3:00 p.m., I was there the next morning at 6:15, eager to start work at $6.00 an hour—way above the $2.15 minimum wage at the time.

Most residents were age eighty and up. I helped them walk around the corridor, gave them their medication, fed them, helped them go to the bathroom, picked up their bedpans, bathed them—and listened to their stories.

Most of them were educated, successful professionals. But now, at the end of their journey, they were frail, insecure, shy, isolated, and some were terribly unloved. Kids and grandkids would come once in a while. But most residents would tell me their kids were too busy, too far away, or they just couldn't be bothered. These patients had sold their homes and had comfortable bank accounts, but they said it didn't make a difference.

"Our kids are waiting for us to go, so they can get rich," they would say.

I would calm them down with words of wisdom from some secret place in my heart; I simply didn't know where it was coming from. But because I was (and still am) very close to my own mother, this understanding felt totally natural.

In the three months I worked at the convalescent center, I was moved from resident care to the kitchen, where I taught the chef some Hungarian dishes, cleaned vegetables, cut the meat, served meals, cleaned tables, and mopped dining room and kitchen floors.

Throughout those three months, I continued to look for work in my field. When I was hired as assistant controller for a clothing manufacturer, I was ecstatic.

Looking back, I'm so grateful for the nursing home experience. It gave me a profound understanding about life, physical work, and the need to be compassionate and LISTEN. The elderly people had so much poise and wisdom! Once in a while, they'd even crack a joke.

When I said goodbye to those wonderful residents and crew, I felt happy for myself, but sad for them. I knew the joy of starting over with hope and faith and a notion of success. But for them, it was the end of the rope: no hope, no goals, and no path to success.

The new company, in North Hollywood, was run by two different partners, each in charge of a division: men's shirts or ladies' casual dresses. One of the founders was from Argentina, and the other was a young African-American man who'd grown up in the South. Though they had different personalities, they agreed on making the company a huge success.

Shirley, the controller, was very happy with my performance, and I became very dedicated to her. I was thrilled to go home with a weekly paycheck and loved my work.

One afternoon, just as I was ready to leave the office, I got up from my chair too quickly. For a second, I put my hand on my lower back.

"What's the matter?" Shirley asked.

"Nothing," I said. "My back is hurting a bit, and the carpet is not as soft as it appears.

"What?!" she screamed out in disbelief. "Are you sleeping on the floor?"

Just then, Mitchell, one of the owners, walked in to hear me answer, "Yes. We still don't have enough money to buy furniture, and we do sleep on the carpet."

"No employee of mine will sleep on the floor," Mitchell exclaimed. He handed me his credit card for Wickes Furniture. "Go over there this weekend and purchase all the furniture you need. I will authorize the transaction. This is your early Christmas bonus—you deserve it."

I couldn't speak. Tears rolled down my face. It was a miracle that I still deeply appreciate decades later.

And then, Mitchell smiled at me. "By the way, Ana, I will collect for my generosity. We need your help on the line, arranging the clothing for the shows next week. We've been watching you, the clothes you wear. They look expensive; you choose rich fabrics. Carlos wants you to take a look at the fabrics he is purchasing, and Helen wants to show you the designs for the next season."

I'd learned about fabric quality from my father, a leading designer of men's suits, jackets, and topcoats in Europe. My grandfather had noticed early on that my father was drawn to the sewing machine—he'd taken several of his father's jackets apart and reassembled them with different stitching—and so he'd sent my father out as a young man to study clothing design in Switzerland.

Wow!

"Yes, of course! I can help anywhere, as long as Shirley is okay with it—or perhaps I should work overtime?"

Indeed, I did work overtime and on the weekends, too. I felt abundant, efficient, and very much appreciated.

In the garment industry—to me, a complex new world—everything is driven by absolute deadlines. Production for each season has to be done six months ahead; summer dresses have to be presented at shows in the winter and early spring. Inventory, workflow, and distribution have to be set before the company even knows if the product will sell. Like any entrepreneurial venture, it's a bit of a gamble. At this position, I learned how to make sure the odds are in your favor.

Working for Shirley in accounting, I was assigned to make collection calls to all the major department stores and a few smaller clothing stores around the country: Sears, Broadway, JC Penney, Alexander's...

And I collected well. I built relationships; I worked with the customers on weekly installment payments; and I worked with "factoring companies" that buy unpaid invoices at a discount. I enjoyed my responsibilities.

Better yet, I was able to help the design department with a few clean and chic dress ideas, and I was instrumental in helping Carlos purchase better fabrics. In the long run, the higher cost of materials was justified, because the good fabrics were easier to work with (saving labor costs)—and the quality delighted our customers.

Within a year, the company had moved to a larger facility and built additional offices for the management staff. I felt that my work in collections, design, and purchasing all contributed to this great success.

CHAPTER 10

Marvelous Marble

Takeaway Tools:

- **Change.** Change can be a great thing. Always be ready to see the opportunity that change presents. I had to overcome my own initial resistance to switching careers, and discovered an opportunity that was better in every way.
- **Service.** Fabulous customer service yields terrific results. As you improve your relationship with customers and prospects, you automatically improve your relationship with money.
- **Relationships.** Building relationships is directly related to building a successful business and a positive cash flow.

New opportunities show up in the strangest places!

As I stood in the check-out line at the supermarket, with my little basket containing only a loaf of bread, butter, and a carton of eggs, the woman behind me smiled. "It looks like you have all of the essentials for a good breakfast—or any meal."

"Oh, yes," I replied. "My family loves this bread, and we all felt like having omelets for dinner." My mouth watered as I thought of toasting the bread and buttering it to go with our omelets and a delicious Israeli salad. We had the vegetables at home for the simple salad: chopped tomatoes, cucumbers, onions, a dash of salt, a little olive oil, and maybe some pepper, a few drops of lemon or a splash of vinegar. It was a delicious addition to any meal, and it was a favorite salad in our house.

The woman asked me about my accent, and I told her I spoke several languages, but I was born in Romania. I also happened to mention that I'd worked for several international businesses. Immediately, her interest grew. "We are both European!" she beamed. "I am from Norway."

Her next question took me completely by surprise.

"Are you looking for work, by any chance? My husband owns a marble company, and he is looking for a new controller."

The controller had suddenly decided to retire early and move back to the East Coast to be closer to her family.

I was flattered, but I really wasn't looking for work. "No," I answered. "Thank you very much, but I am happy with my current job."

The woman was undeterred. She asked a few more polite questions. "You know, you are just the kind of person we are looking for. Where do you work?"

I told her about the clothing manufacturing company, where I was putting in 50- to 55-hour weeks, including time on weekends.

"Your current job is quite different than the marble business," she admitted. "But I just have a feeling you are exactly who we need. I bet you would adjust quickly—and what would you think about working fewer hours for more money?"

Now she had my attention! My son was still small, and after many months of soul searching, I was considering dissolving my marriage. Fewer hours in the office would give me more time with Sean and help us both make the difficult personal adjustment that loomed ahead of us. It also made more sense geographically, as it was only a few blocks from Sean's school.

I agreed to meet with Liv's husband, the company president.

On the day of our interview, an incredible sense of calm and rightness washed over me. If he offered me the job, I would trust my common sense and the personal reality that I needed more time and money, and take it. And so it happened.

I immediately told my boss, Shirley, and the owners of the clothing company. They were all sad to see me go, but they understood my reasons and were genuinely happy for me. The road was clear for my next adventure in the business world.

I began working for the marble company one week later, working only 40 hours and making $100 extra every week— big money back then! It was actually odd at first to adjust to a schedule that didn't include all that overtime and grueling deadlines. I joined my first 401k plan, and the company matched 20 percent. It was a big step up for me in so many ways—and the most exciting was another chance to learn an entirely new and very intriguing business.

Our customers were home and commercial property designers, architects, builders, contractors, and some private clients. We purchased marble, granite, onyx, grout, tile and other materials from Italy, Greece, Pakistan, Turkey, Spain, Portugal, and India. The company imported huge slabs, along with finished marble tiles, so we were always eager to greet a new shipment. My international business experience both at the exporting company in New York and the maritime bank in Israel came in very handy as I learned this new milieu.

Every business has its own particular motion and vocabulary, and I quickly learned about the differences between the materials we sold, the value in the thickness, color, vein, and the trick to cutting quality pieces. Then I tackled the related world of interior design.

It was exhilarating, and I enjoyed it tremendously. Within a year, I was not only working as the controller, but also selling, meeting with designers, and supporting the sales team. I was a constant advocate for creativity and continuous improvement.

As my job expanded, my mission became simpler: to build relationships and trust. I advised clients on their choices and let them know right up front if certain materials were out of stock and when they'd be replenished. Our goals were always delighted clients and projects completed correctly and on time.

Business flourished. By the second year, we'd reduced our debt, hired a few more employees, and increased our client base. Customer trust and satisfaction was through the roof, because our clients knew that we'd always go the extra mile for them.

When we didn't have the answers or the materials they needed, we sent them to our local competitor. Although that shocked quite a few clients, it made good business sense. We were there to provide exceptional service, and sometimes that meant sending them across town to someone who could help. And not surprisingly, our competitor frequently reciprocated many times. Our approach worked beautifully for everyone involved—especially the customer.

We also designed a beautiful showroom. This was by no means a frivolous expense. They could see and touch our products, get ideas for creative ways to use them, and find out what to match with what, how to place certain colors next to each other, and why sometimes an understated look was more attractive.

So an ordinary day in the supermarket led to an incredible business opportunity and a chance to strengthen my friendship with money. From that point on, I knew that I should always be ready for change—and welcome it with open arms. I don't think the company president was ever sorry that his wife stopped to chat with me in the grocery store. And neither was I!

CHAPTER 11

Food, glorious finance

Take Away Tools:

- **Perishable Inventory.** Inventory rules are different when you have to throw things away if they're not used within a few days.
- **Juggling and Multitasking.** In a restaurant business, if you can only do one thing at a time, you will be out of business very quickly. I learned to juggle setting shift schedules, delighting customers, keeping costs down, and cultivating a happy environment for our employees.

My four years working for the marble company were packed with learning and change. I immersed myself in a completely new business; I got divorced; and I married a man who taught at the local university part-time. My new husband also helped to run his family's Mexican restaurant.

His mother had built the family restaurant from nothing to a thriving business, and their customers loved them. Because the restaurant only seated eighteen people, most of the business was take-out. Eventually, the family decided to expand. They needed space to accommodate their customers who wanted to dine in, and they also wanted to maintain the thriving take-out side of the business.

When I realized that my husband could really use my help in this new venture, I decided to leave my job at the marble company. Though I was sad to leave such a wonderful business, with colleagues who had become friends, I wanted to try my luck at entrepreneurship, and the restaurant business was very appealing to me. I knew this project wouldn't last forever, but nevertheless, I was happy to flow with the change and learn another new business.

But everything builds on what came before, and one never completely says goodbye. The marble business was wonderfully connected to the restaurant business.

The marble company taught me how to design and create an attractive environment, and my expertise proved very useful as the family created their new restaurant just two doors down from the old one. We purchased the building from a jeweler who had recently gone out of business—and we bought the tile, marble, and other materials from the marble company. Everything came together beautifully, and soon we were looking at a lovely, homey restaurant that seated about 100 people, with additional seating for 150 in a party room. We had also designed a sleek bar area.

This was an exciting time for all of us. It was new territory for the entire family. My husband resigned from his teaching job and became the operations manager and chef. He loved to cook and learned his mother's famous recipes very quickly.

The food was authentic and delicious—never heavy. It was just right. The quantities were generous and beautifully presented; more importantly, we kept the prices reasonable, and the service impeccable. I still remember the delicious smell of soups simmering in the kitchen. Our best was the albondiga (meatball) soup, but on Sunday mornings, our menudo (tripe) soups were always in high demand. On Mother's Day, Easter, and Christmas we prepared hundreds of tamales for take-out and eat-in guests.

It was a busy, happy time for all of us. Everyone was so excited to see the new restaurant succeed. All family members pitched in to make it work. We sat down together and developed this list of priorities:

1. Fresh produce daily
2. Highest quality meats and fish
3. Tasty foods
4. Valued employees who would never have more than two to three consecutive shifts
5. Cross-training in the kitchen
6. Friendly and excellent service
7. Good prices
8. Clean walls, floors, and chairs

It was wonderful to be a part of our restaurant team. Our one little business gave many families their bread and butter and a roof over their head, and that felt good. Customers would drive from as far north as Santa Barbara and as far south as San Diego to get a meal at our restaurant. We booked events throughout the year—sweet-sixteen parties; quinceañeras, weddings, and anniversaries. People wanted to spend special days with us. We were proud of what we had created together.

My life instantly became more colorful. It felt amazing to apply skills I'd learned in other businesses to this new trade. Building on the visual presentation skills I'd learned working first in the garment industry and then in interior decorating at the marble company, I discovered the power of presentation, taste, and quality of food. I also learned to admire and appreciate the beauty of Mexican cooking through the various dishes we served on a regular basis: steak picado, chile rellenos, carne asada, camarones con papas, and of course, our famous chicken, rice, and bean burritos and huevos rancheros.

I love Mexican food, and I still eat it quite often. Every time I pick up a menu in a Mexican restaurant or bite into a spicy meal, I have a flashback to those beautiful, colorful days. The taste is bittersweet today but I still savor it.

CHAPTER 12

10,000 percent growth

Takeaway Tools:

- **Thin is Not In.** Don't spread yourself too thin. Focus on specific products in a specific geographic area and build your reputation.
- **Commitment.** Meet all of your commitments with honor and respect.
- **Extra Mile.** Going the extra mile with quality products and effort will always pay off.
- **Building Relationships Outside of Work.** It's not always just about business. The Passover feast was one of many chances I had to build relationships with my employer's family. In every job where I've reached out, all the way back to Mrs. Schechter, it's been a good thing.

After the restaurant became successful, I was again free to pursue my own business interests. My next experience in the business world was again completely new; this time, I became controller for a just-launched commercial building and construction company.

Like me, the owner had come to the United States as a young person, determined to succeed. He'd immigrated to the U.S. at age twenty-three with $1,000 cash in his pocket and nothing else. He had no immediate family in the States, just a few friends and one or two distant cousins. Also like me, he'd also originally planned to live in New York, but found California was more fertile ground.

I deeply enjoyed working for this young, dynamic gentleman. He was hungry to build a reputation in the construction world, had an innocent look and a huge smile that made people trust him, and shared my own values and strategies for success. Everyone liked him.

Our first step in building his business was to decide what to focus on. He would specialize in one or two types of projects—and would stay local. Then he would really get to know his customer base and build a solid reputation.

This strategy paid off. He landed jobs building local schools and shopping centers. He loved his work—and his passion shone through in every aspect of every job. He hired top-notch builders and experienced foremen to oversee the projects. Rain or shine, the jobs were completed on time—some of them ahead of schedule.

And the quality of his work was excellent. Inferior materials were not an option. He knew they would slow progress and ruin his reputation in the construction world. Instead, he chose the best in every area, and we actually came out ahead. We shopped around and chose high-quality materials from reliable vendors at honest prices. We built strong relationships at every point in the process, and the result was a great reputation and a flood of work.

Word got out that his business was one of the best in the area. People also heard about his spectacular follow-through. Customers could contact him anytime if they needed anything from a bolt to a new door handle to installing an elevator. No follow-up project was too big or small. This guy didn't drop out of sight as soon as he was paid his final invoice.

The malls he developed were popular, and the schools he remodeled were also in perfect shape. Customer satisfaction was high, and he continually had repeat customers. I used to visit the job sites, because they inspired me. I loved seeing the progress we made week after week.

Miraculously, as the company grew, our stress decreased. We grew from $100,000 to $12 million in just three years. We also set up a healthy cash flow by requiring a 33 percent deposit at the start of each job and then progress billing (sending invoices as we reached agreed milestones) throughout the contract.

It was a terrific learning experience for me, too, because my job became quite diversified. I covered the billing, reconciliations, financial statements, collections, bids, and payroll. I even talked with inspectors. After a few years, I felt like I could do it all!

Something else special happened at this company. Even though it was outside of my formal job description, it had a significant impact on my desire to build relationships and go the extra mile.

I had developed a close relationship with the owner's family. I got along very well with his wife and young son, and they had another child on the way. When I'd been there about a year, and Passover was approaching, they invited twenty-three people for dinner to their Passover Seder dinner.

Of course, by this point, they knew that I loved to cook. Still, I was amazed when the owners asked me if I would prepare the holiday feast. This was not a simple favor. They gave me several days off to prepare, doubled my pay during that time, and gave me a $500 bonus. I was thrilled.

Thanks to my experiences at Kibbutz Mossad, the convalescent home, and my family's restaurant, I knew how to cook for a crowd. I prepared the menu, and they approved it and purchased the ingredients. It was a superb evening, and I couldn't stop smiling when everyone attending asked if they could take some leftovers home.

You might get a kick out of the menu for the evening:

- Homemade gefilte fish (salmon and whitefish ground with grilled onions, garlic, shredded carrots, and shredded almonds) formed in the shape of large, flat meatballs and chilled, served with cooked carrots, onions, and potatoes
- Chicken and turkey soup with vegetables and matzah balls (ground matzah—a no-yeast flatbread eaten on Passover, when regular breads are forbidden—with eggs, salt, and pepper; they look like round dumplings, and are cooked in boiling hot soup or water)
- Eggplant salad (chopped, baked eggplant with thin-cut purple onions, olive oil, and fresh lemon juice)
- Israeli salad (chopped cucumbers, onions, parsley, and tomatoes with olive oil, lots of lemon, and a dash of honey)
- Egg and avocado salad (cooked eggs, chopped green onions, and chopped avocado with salt, pepper, and Hungarian paprika
- Beef pot roast
- Goulash (Hungarian-style veal with potatoes)
- Stuffed cabbage with rice, ground turkey, and chicken
- Baked turkey
- Baked yams
- Portobello mushrooms with a glazed sweet-and-sour sauce. Lots of good wine and mineral water
- Baked apples with caramel sauce
- Baked peaches, apricots, and pears with honey and whipped cream
- Dark chocolate-filled Passover wafers
- Coffee and tea

What a feast! I still remember that event so clearly. I've had many wonderful Passover and High Holiday dinners, but that one was in the top five. I'll always cherish the memory of that evening.

CHAPTER 13

Holding spacecraft together—while my life fell apart

Takeaway Tools:

- **Adjust.** Both in business and in your personal life, be flexible and willing to adjust. In the spacecraft industry, I had to adjust product innovations to meet market needs, and I had to adjust our manufacturing schedule to meet demand. I learned to adjust when a natural disaster crashed through my home and the business I expected to run, too. Nothing ever stays the same. When you can go with the flow, you'll ride out any storm.
- **Create Alignment.** Alignment is crucial for any successful business: you must align your products and services with your market, align your employees with your company's mission, and align your business mission with a higher purpose.Our success in the aerospace industry increased dramatically once we were able to align our company's capabilities with the right market segment.
- **Solve Problems.** Whatever situation you're in, in any industry—be a problem solver. People want to work with someone who will bring solutions to the table, not whine about the problems. In this part of my life, I first had the problem of a boss who didn't think he wanted me in the position, and then the many problems that always surface when a company grows so rapidly. In my own life, I faced the compound problem of suddenly being homeless and

watching my savings transform into debt. Both at work and at home, I focused on how to make the situation better.

- **Pricing.** The more you know about how a business works, the more valuable you are as an employee, a manager, or an owner/entrepreneur. I immersed myself in first understanding, and then refining, our pricing strategy, and that was part of our success and growth.
- **Motivation.** Inspire the people around you! Employees need a reason to come in to work every day; if all they get is a paycheck and a boatload of problems, your profitability is at risk. But when you show them that you greatly value not just their labor but their ideas, they will be there for you. Their productivity will increase, and when you need to hire, they'll even recruit their friends and family (which lowers your costs enormously, by the way). When you cultivate relationships with employees and coworkers, the feeling that we're all in this together motivates them to do more.

Life is never static, and I think that's great. Things change constantly—sometimes in a way that's obviously good (such as when I went from the convalescent home to the clothing company and then to the marble firm)—but sometimes in ways that feel pretty rough at the time.

Later—sometimes years later—I look back and see how those challenges made room for amazing joys and opportunities down the road. But while the crises were happening, I did my share of weeping and wailing and grieving. Even after spiraling so far toward success, I had a couple of years where it was all I could do just to hold everything together. Maybe it was appropriate that my job at the time had to do with just that—holding things together, particularly spacecraft.

This new venture was my first experience in manufacturing: producing electric motors and encoders for medical and aerospace customers. I was hired as a controller, and I helped to build the company from 7 employees and $250,000 a year to $62 million a year and 83 new full-time positions. It's rare to be part of that kind of monumental growth, and I was thrilled.

But it almost didn't happen. My first interview at the company was not a success. Even though he himself was a Hungarian immigrant with a strong accent, the president had ordered his human resources manager not to employ any foreigners with accents. Under the circumstances, it was surprising that I'd even gotten an interview.

The HR manager complied with his directive; they interviewed and hired one controller after another, but every one of them failed. They had a terrible time finding a good fit for the job. Finally, the president gave in. He remembered my interview, and even though I was a European and had an accent, he decided to give me a try.

So, right from the beginning, I knew it was going to be a challenge. I had to bring my very best to the table. I knew deep down that I was the right one for the job, and our success proved me right. The company president and I became the best of friends. We did tremendous research and by doing so we aligned our products to meet the demand. The area we were concentrating on was in the medical field, how to improve the blood analyzers for testing's, the breathing machines and turned towards the sleep apnea field and to the aerospace industry. We built in-house equipment to cut back on labor cost and timing and therefore we were able to come up with great pricing and meet the demand. We create exclusivity and that by itself increased the overall business and profit margins. This was a niche business. Of course, our success didn't happen overnight. I had to gradually gain the trust of my coworkers, and then together we built the company one block at a time. Slowly, our hard work bore fruit, and that propelled us on to ever-larger goals.

This was a happy time for me. I was "jazzed" by the company's rapid growth, and I enjoyed a wonderful personal life, as well. My son had grown into a strong and capable young man, about to graduate from college. Sean was excited about his future and brimming with ideas and plans.

Money had become a very good friend of mine by this time in my life. We'd moved into a lovely home in Sherman Oaks, California, which I saw as the perfect opportunity to feed my creative passions; of course, I launched into a major remodel of the house.

Our new home was a beautiful reflection of everything I had learned over the years. Three-fourths of the house was encased in 20-foot glass walls, and our marble entryway guided visitors to an illuminated winter garden with rocks that had been collected from around the world.

I loved to entertain, so we had a white formal dining room that spilled out into a huge Japanese-garden-style backyard with a large pool area and a Jacuzzi. We could easily accommodate up to 120 people outside.

Inside our home, every detail was hand-picked and of the highest quality. I had marble and Italian tile bathrooms, a lovely kitchen with white and light-yellow diamond designs, and brand-new, gleaming, white appliances. The walls were painted in shades ranging from light yellow to lavender, peach, and apple green. My son's bathroom was decorated with jade tile floors. The home was my masterpiece—a breathtaking collection of all that I had learned about design, fashion, and quality materials.

My husband and I continued to help with his family restaurant, even though I'd moved on to other corporate challenges full-time. Our relationship went through several shifts during this period, too. We divorced, but remained close friends. Then we changed our minds! He moved back in with me, and we began building a life together all over again. After we reunited, we decided that it would be wonderful to build our own restaurant close to our haven in Sherman Oaks.

Just down the street from us, we found a huge lot with an existing building. We began with blueprints and let our creativity go wild to create an innovative space where we would serve Mediterranean food with a touch of Mexican flair. We'd include some European dishes, as well.

My son Sean got involved too. He purchased cobalt blue glass blocks for the restaurant, similar to those in our home. Investing all our time and money into this project, we took out home equity loans to hire the contractor. Our dream was forming right on schedule, and it really united us as a family.

But adversity lurked just around the corner.

On January 17, 1994, at 4:31 in the morning, a few rocky minutes changed everything. The Northridge Earthquake shattered dishes and glasses as they spilled out of cabinets, and crumbled and cracked our glass walls; I'll never forget the terrible sights and sound of that night.

And our dreams were shattered as well.

The restaurant location was hit hard, too. We had no earthquake insurance, and because both of us had a good income, we didn't qualify for aid. We were forced to give up the restaurant and turn in the keys to our dream home to the bank. We had no cash left to rebuild either one.

It was heartbreaking for all of us to close that fairytale chapter of our lives, but we chose not to dwell on the destruction. Instead, we concentrated on what we were grateful for. While we had lost our home and our dreams, none of us was hurt in the earthquake. And we had each other, our families, and very good jobs. Instead of trying to hold the rubble together, we held on to each other and moved on.

Life is a roller-coaster ride; I learn this universal lesson over and over. But life is a good teacher, too. It shows us that any of us can be on top of the world one minute and at the bottom of the heap the next, shaking and afraid that we will never be able to rise again. But we will. We can. We do rise again!

Sean decided to go back to school and get his MBA. Now, he is Vice President, Oracle Worldwide Practice and CFO advisory services. I've found my calling as a speaker, writer, and entrepreneur. I often wonder what would have happened if our restaurant venture had succeeded; perhaps Sean would never have found his true passion, for computers and world finance—and I would not be talking to you right now about your higher purpose and future wealth.

Sean married in 1997. Then he and his wife gave me one of the greatest gifts ever: grandchildren! Logan and Mia are pure light in my life. They're not only my grandchildren, but my sweetest friends. We share stories (mostly fiction), but sometimes I tell them a little bit about my crazy, beautiful life, and they eat it up.

As I'm writing this book, Sean is grieving the death of his father (my first husband). He was a good, kind, and quiet man, who taught my son to follow his passions.

The earthquake in 1994 shook us to our core—but, looking back, it was one of the best things that happened to us. Yes, money flowed away with that tragedy, and we had to struggle for a while. But it came back to us in ways we could never have predicted, and we were ultimately strengthened by the experience. Today, I consult on finance to companies all over the world; I'm an international public speaker; I conduct workshops; and I get to share my story of how a poor girl from Romania can end up a successful entrepreneur in sunny California.

And now, I'm married to Mario Haber, an amazing, supportive, loving, and brilliant man. He has two grown daughters, and we all fit together seamlessly, as if we were puzzle pieces that were always meant to connect.

My mother, who has shared so many struggles and triumphs with me along the way, is now 95. She is a woman of substance, who taught me to never give up. Together, we've forged ahead, regardless of the obstacles in our way. And here we are, smiling as we greet each new day! I am so grateful for her strength and her love.

I've learned that life never stays the same. I don't have to try to hold the pieces together. It's okay to release them and follow the flow. That is when I am open to reaching new and unexpected heights.

CHAPTER 14

Signs of progress

Takeaway Tools:

- **Embrace Opportunity.** Never say no to an opportunity to shine.
- **Support.** Always give support. Help your customers, vendors, and friends when they face challenges. Offer a helping hand when they need it the most. Help people, without preconditions, and your deeds will double in power.
- **The Universe Times it Right.** Even if it doesn't seem that way at first, when you take the long view, the larger pattern will work itself out. Eventually, you'll be in exactly the right place at the right time.
- **Be Efficient.** Manage your time and your staff's time efficiently. Put your company in a position to get things done.
- **Analyze.** Look carefully at the entire picture. You'll find additional opportunities for your organization.
- **Be Secure.** Feel secure and comfortable in your company position. Be willing to stand your ground when you know you offer the best products or services.
- **Motivate Your Employees.** Motivate your staff, and guide them to understand and share in the success of the company.

The signs of progress aren't always clear at first, but eventually they materialize. I was feeling itchy for a change, a new challenge—but I had no idea where it would show up. It finally came with an offer to be controller at an architectural sign company.

I'd known this company and its executives for many years; they'd given my first husband his first job in California. He'd been an excellent controller in Israel, but his weak command of English had made it a struggle to find a job in the United States. When he'd applied to work in the finance department back in 1975, one of the owners hired him to work in purchasing. It was a great match—and a huge relief.

Years later, as I began looking for a new opportunity, they needed a controller. Not only did it feel like the right job and another step up the career ladder, but it also gave me a chance to pay back their kindness years earlier. They gave me a huge office with a large window, and everyone was friendly and cooperative. I knew right away that I'd made a smart move.

I really enjoyed this job. They already had a terrific reputation among large hotels, shopping centers, corporate offices, and even billboard companies around the world. We processed a tremendous quantity of bids each month and our very solid sales team followed up intelligently and promptly.

One day, the company president happened to mention that he'd love to win a bid from the Smithsonian Institute in Washington (America's national museum complex).

"What's stopping you?" I asked.

He laughed. One of our biggest competitors had been working for the Smithsonian for years. They had a track record with the organization, a good price point, and an established and comfortable relationship. The president of our company saw little chance of us elbowing our way into that opportunity.

"You never know," I smiled. "Don't give up."

Just a few weeks later, the Smithsonian sent us a bid request. Our team put the bid aside, assuming there was no point in creating a quote if we had little to no chance of getting it.

When I heard the news, I insisted (politely) that they put in a bid. I also took several additional steps on my own. Here's what I did:

- Personally followed up on the quote
- Reached out to the decision maker at the Smithsonian
- Extended additional support with financial planning for architectural changes, including maintaining their flow of visitors
- Suggested extending incentives to visitors to make a visit worthwhile, despite the inconvenience of certain exhibits being closed for construction
- Offered unconditional follow-up to streamline the schedule, meet financial demands, respond to visitor demands, and monitor construction progress. I showed how this follow-up procedure would increase visitors, create more revenue, make more time for construction changes, and meet all expenses—which would in turn reduce management stress and the need to borrow

When Maryanne, my contact, showed the Smithsonian board members my intense financial spreadsheets, how I anticipated and solved problems, and how I'd worked to create the very best scenario and results, they were astounded.

"I think this is a company you would want to award the job to with a smile, don't you?" she asked.

Indeed, they did. We got the job!

After two decades of trying, we finally had a contract from the Smithsonian—and everyone in the company was thrilled. And we came through with flying colors. The project was a major success, and I added another title after my name: Ana Weber, Financial Controller and VP of Sales.

I learned something very important from this experience: people fear success more than they fear failure. You have to follow up on success. If you're chosen, you have to deliver with flying colors. If you fail, the work is over. But which would you truly prefer? Success and unlimited potential for growth—or failure, eventual stagnation, and death? It's not a hard choice.

Since that experience, I've learned to stay very close to the sales management team—the beating heart of a business—at every company I've worked for. Whenever we experience tough times, we look back at logs and purchase orders and dig into the sales numbers to find ordering patterns. This gives me clues to both extend a deep appreciation for existing business (which often generates more business just from saying thank-you)—and to unearth more business opportunities by studying the histories and trends.

CHAPTER 15

Racing porsches, racing numbers

Takeaway Tools:

- **Safety.** Safety is crucial—especially when speeding along over 100 miles an hour!
- **Balance.** When serving more than one master, sometimes you have to juggle. I learned to balance Porsche's rigid standards with each customer's uniqueness. And I also learned just how important it is to slow down enough to savor the best moments and stop to recharge along the way. The journey is just as important as the finish line.
- **Loyalty.** Loyalty is important, even when things don't turn out as planned—a lesson I'd known instinctively all the way back to the day at my very first job when I told Mrs. Schechter I'd stay long enough to hire and train my replacement. The importance of loyalty was brought home to me when I remained loyal to my husband and followed him to a new location, leaving behind a successful business and starting over yet again. While our marriage ultimately didn't last, my loyalty opened new and thrilling chapters in my life. Sometimes you CAN'T have it all, and you have to make choices. I had to choose between keeping my marriage and keeping my wonderful job. Ironically, by choosing my marriage, I ended up without a marriage for a while, but with an even better career.
- **Real Satisfaction.** Given a car worth more than $100,000, I quickly discovered that the pleasure was fleeting. Real happiness is not built on flashy luxuries, but on the things

> that really matter: friends, loved ones, good times, good food, new places and experiences...and on having a passion for life so you enjoy almost all of it.

Life zoomed on, and soon enough, I found an entirely new set of challenges. As both Financial Controller and VP of Sales, I'd achieved a lot at the architectural company. But my third marriage brought me to a new crossroads.

Although I was thriving in this job, my new husband really wanted to move to Orange County. An avid diver, he wished to take advantage of the beautiful weather in the San Fernando Valley. Looking back, I realize that he didn't really respect my identity as a businesswoman or my desire to stay with that company. But it was still my decision to go with him to Orange County, keep our marriage, leave my business, and start over again in a new company.

This series of decisions seemed to take me off track. But actually, my career was shifting into high gear, as life got even more exciting: Porsche hired me as a controller in their race car division.

Talk about exhilarating! This new world literally ran at over 100 miles per hour. In my new industry, safety was paramount—our number-one concern at every moment. And all of the paperwork we submitted was ultra-detailed, from the engineering specs to the methodical German-style financial statements. Porsche was built on precision, and everything we did reflected that.

But we also paid attention to each client's unique needs and desires. Every driver was different, and even the race courses had their own idiosyncrasies. We sold race cars to numerous celebrities, including the president of AT&T, and we took personal care with each client.

Porsche exposed me to the wonderful world of racing—but that fast-paced world also taught me that there was no benefit to speeding through life. I had to make a conscious effort to find time to stop and smell the roses.

One day, I looked around and realized that not all of our Porsche executives drove Porsches! That looked like bad marketing to me, so I wrote to Porsche headquarters in Stuttgart, Germany that I believed management should back their own products and only drive Porsches.

Headquarters was quick to respond to my request. They sent everyone on our management team a custom-made Porsche directly from Germany. Mine was a Carrera with soft, luxurious seats and a beautiful taupe exterior. At first, I got quite a lift driving around in my new, fancy car, reveling in the admiring glances that floated my way as I roared down the street. However, like all materialistic toys, the fun was fleeting and the novelty wore off. I learned that even the finest luxury goods never bring true happiness and contentment—but it was fun for a short while!

After a few years, I left Porsche. My husband worked as a consultant and general manager for a washer company in Gardena, and when their controller resigned with no notice, he panicked and begged me to take on the position. Together we organized the department, automated the books, and made some other significant improvements.

As it turned out, my husband and I split up in 2006.*For the very first time in my life*, I had to find a place to live on my own. I gave up our home and started fresh in a rental unit. I was fifty-five years old and an independent woman again!

While the marriage didn't last, my position did. I've now been a consultant there for over ten years, and I continue to help the company stay strong, even in a struggling economy. This position gives me the freedom to pursue my newest passions: writing books and articles about personal growth, speaking and teaching programs, and appearing regularly on television and radio, and in newspaper and magazine articles. I live my dreams today, because I followed the flow of life and threw myself into each new opportunity with the optimism and energy that only genuine passion can bring.

CHAPTER 16

WASHING AWAY DEBT (AND TRIPLING SALES)

Takeaway Tools:

- **Customize.** The same solution won't work for everyone. I learned to build separate and honorable terms with different vendors and customers.
- **Keep Your Commitments.** Always meet your commitments! Our reputation was built on our terrific follow-through.
- **Harness the Relationships You Build.** Once you've built strong relationships, you can leverage them to create positive money flow. When we developed positive relationships with our bankers, we had more options to reduce our debt.
- **Pay Upfront.** For long-term financial health, it's often much smarter to purchase machinery and other equipment with cash, not loans—especially if the company is already in debt.
- **Add Value.** I'll say it again: the best way to be successful is to make fabulous products, delivered on time, and at a good price. Make quality a priority and your business will grow and thrive.

When I joined the washer manufacturing company in 2002, my original task was to reorganize the accounting department and automate the washer company's entire accounting system—and you can imagine what kind of accounting "system" I'd inherited from a controller who left without notice.

While this was no small job, I quickly realized that this was only the beginning.

The company was awash with millions of dollars of debt. I had to not only learn—and then replace—all the systems, but also wash away that debt and turn this business from negative to positive money flow.

The thought of it could have been overwhelming, but I concentrated on making everything simpler while increasing control over the accounting practices.

First, I designed numerous spreadsheets for each financial area: cash flow; daily and monthly sales; payroll; banking credit lines; projections, etc.

Once I had each area organized, I developed a very cool system to set different payment schedules and credit terms for each class of customers and vendors (freight, raw materials, etc.). I left nothing up to chance. At first, I shortened terms to customers and extended the time before paying vendors just to turn around the money flow. I also introduced a credit card system that lengthened our expense flow cycle just a bit. This middle transaction gave us additional time to improve our cash flow, and of course, I paid the corporate credit card balances in full before their due date, because credit card interest is a very expensive way to rent money.

I also opened a merchant account that allowed our own customers to pay with credit cards. And if certain reliable customers needed extended terms, we would extend credit out to 30 to 55 days.

By changing the direction of our money flow while offering more options to customers, our relationships with customers, vendors, and the banks made a significant shift. We were now seen as a reputable and honorable company—and we built on that reputation to wash away our debt and increase our sales.

I played with time and money to create a more positive cash flow. In the end, we were able to eliminate $3 million in debt and triple our annual sales from $10 million to $30 million per year.

I'm still a consultant with this company, and because of our robust money flow system, we are still doing fantastically, despite the downturn in the economy. No debt, no worries, and no cash flow problems whatsoever.

CHAPTER 17

AUDITS DON'T HAVE TO BE AWFUL—IF YOU'RE ALREADY ORGANIZED

Takeaway Tools:

- **Make Friends with Apparent Enemies.** Don't let yourself be intimidated. Even if the IRS knocks at your door, befriend your auditors. Work alongside them and help them as much as you can. Remember, they're people, too, and they're just doing their job. A side benefit: if auditors or other people in positions of authority like and respect you, they'll treat you more kindly. On the other hand, if you make their lives difficult, they have the power to make your life a living hell.
- **Get Organized.** When your firm is well-organized, you'll lower stress and increase productivity—and you'll be prepared for unexpected events, from an audit to a potential buy-out.
- **Embrace Transparency.** If you're open about your business processes, and have kept good records that you can easily locate, you have much less to fear.
- **Appreciate.** Show appreciation to the auditor for teaching you good systems to maintain financial accuracy and financial health. Show appreciation for your employees, because they are the lifeblood of your company.
- **Reduce Stress.** Keep your workplace as stress-free as possible. Stress never made anyone more productive. If you develop a well-organized business, inside and out, you'll

eliminate a lot of stress and create the freedom for you and your employees to do your jobs unencumbered.

Everything was humming along. The company had gotten rid of our debt, and profits were steadily climbing. Then in 2006, the one piece of mail every company dreads showed up in my inbox: a letter from the IRS. We would be fully audited in three weeks, and they were demanding to see a list of 26 items. My heart sank.

What do you do when you receive this kind of news? If you're like me, first you panic. But then you still have to deal with it. Deep down, I knew we had nothing to be worried about; we'd done a lot of work to organize the business, and all of that hard work was about to pay off. We had the answers the IRS was seeking, and could account for every aspect of our business.

I immediately began building a respectful relationship with our auditor, starting by politely (and successfully) requesting three more weeks to pull together the information they requested.

The audit actually went beautifully. It was so devoid of stress that I actually became friends with our auditor! We continue to share a friendship and keep up-to-date on what is going on in each other's lives.

This is what work and business is all about: building successful relationships; getting the job done; being accountable; and learning and growing in the process.

Two things saved us: First, we'd put in the time to build systems and effective organizational tools that not only helped us function day to day, but were part of the tremendous turnaround from debt to success; we used these same tools to prepare for and pass the audit. And second, we made it a priority to properly document every aspect. Our business was solid and transparent, and we had nothing to hide from the IRS.

If you ever become a business manager or owner, you may find some of these organizational tools valuable—think of the rest of this chapter as a Management 101 mini-course at no extra cost. Note that "you" in the list below refers to your company. Even if a particular issue isn't your personal responsibility, you should know who's in charge of each step. We'll look first at tools for manufacturers, and then at service business—and then we'll look at the different key roles people take in a successful business:

Manufacturing Companies

- **Customer Quotation Questionnaire.** A simple form that gathers all the specific information you need to prepare a great bid—such as examples, dimensions (including thickness), materials, blueprints, processing, end users, etc. The questionnaire will look different for each business—maybe even for each project. But the goal is consistent: to get all the answers you need to complete the sales process in this first questionnaire. This will save you tons of time as you go through the entire process.

- **Customer Report.** Once the customer turns in the questionnaire, you summarize the answers. This simple report is valuable to both the vendor and the customer, because it solidifies and clarifies needs and expectations. It removes stress, confusion, and misunderstandings, and lets the customer correct any inaccuracies before anyone spends any money.
- **Quote.** Once you have the questionnaire and the customer report, creating the official quote is easy and quick. All the information is already right in front of you. Because it's based in the two earlier documents, your quote will be accurate—and more likely to result in a sale.
- **Purchase Order.** This should also be easy—and should correspond exactly to the quote.
- **Prototype.** Once you have the signed purchase order, you're ready to start work. The next step is to produce a prototype for the customer's approval.
- **Production.** The culmination of all of your preparation: Together with your customer, you've ironed out the details, specified what each side expects from the other, and resolved any issues with the prototype. Now, you're finally ready to go into production and complete the order.
- **Follow-up.** Without being pesky, the right kind of follow-up—based in a sincere desire to be your customer's helper and problem-solver—leads inevitably to repeat sales and referrals. This is what sets strong, successful companies apart from weak, failing ones. Your work is not over when the machines stop running! You'll want to check in several times: Was the shipment received on time and in good order? Is it solving the problem or filling the need that led to the job? How is it holding up over time? Do they need more? Do they also need a different component that you can provide for them? Are their needs changing in ways that could benefit from your help?

Service Businesses

Since services don't need the prototype and production steps of the manufacturing process, they must differentiate themselves on superior **skills/knowledge** and **customer service.**

Customer service is important in any industry, but it's paramount when service *is* the product. Thus, IT companies, restaurants, marketing firms, tourism organizations, financial services groups, and similar organizations must train every staffer not just to provide superior customer service, but to understand its crucial role.

Just as in manufacturing, great follow-up increases customer happiness. Be a problem solver. Connect the customer with the right person who resolves an issue quickly and efficiently, and you've created a customer for life. When you go that extra mile for your customers and your vendors, you'll measure your reward in profits and revenues.

Organizational Chart

Every company or nonprofit needs a strong organizational chart. When job descriptions are clear to workers, management, and customers, the organization is more transparent. This increases credibility, saves time, and clarifies the entire work process. Your organization might use some of these, whether you call them by these other titles:

- CEO – Chief Executive Officer
- CFO – Chief Financial Officer
- Controller/Accounting Manager
- Management
- Marketing
- Sales
- Sustainability Coordinator
- Accounting
- Customer Service
- Human Relations
- Support Team
- Engineering (for manufacturing and other industries, such as architectural firms, design firms, and the bio tech industry)
- Engineering Liaison
- Warehouse
- Stocking
- Receiving
- Shipping
- Returns: Returns and Return Authorizations are essential in any company that sells products. Don't skip this important area; sooner or later, it will demand attention
- Inventory Control
- Quality Control: Nothing should leave the premises without passing through quality control, and quality control needs active encouragement to reject any defective shipment. A terrific

Quality Control department will defend against returns—and maybe a few lawsuits and some bad publicity, too—and keep profits high

- Support (secretaries, assistants, receptionists, filing clerks, etc.)

This list is not intended to be complete, but to get you thinking about your own company's organization. Always develop a structure that fits your company's needs; never try to shoehorn real needs into an unworkable structure just because that structure already exists. In every aspect of your business, think about your goals, and then create a system to advance them. At the same time, don't overdo it. Putting in too rigid a structure too early can kill the entrepreneurial spark and your employees' joy in their work. Make sure your structures actually create space to strengthen your own, your co-workers', and the company's passions—rather than choke them.

And another bit of friendly advice: if at all possible, avoid hiring friends or family members, unless it's a family business. And even then—especially then—make sure you have structures and procedures in place to make it work. This may sound harsh, but friendships and family connections blur the lines; it's much more difficult to manage a friend or family member without giving preferential treatment over other employees. Save yourself a lot of headaches, if you can, and don't hire them in the first place.

But what about if you own a family business? Is it doomed to fail?

Not at all. But you do need to take some specific steps to set boundaries. Leave the family titles at home, and treat each person as an employee—an equal of the organization and a valuable asset—not "Mom" or "Uncle Joe" or "my best friend." And set up an outside, non-family board of advisors who can be objective when you can't.

A Happy Workplace = Higher Profits

We spend more time at work than we do awake at home; shouldn't the largest chunk of our day be as pleasant as possible? Why should anyone have to dread going to work? With that in mind, here are a few more people-management success tips:

Build successful relationships with your employees (there's that *relationship* word again!)—let them know through both actions and words not only how much you value their contribution, but also how much you care about them as human beings. Mrs. Schechter is not a good role model; better to emulate the kindness and generosity of Rachel at the bank and Mitchell at the clothing company.

Make sure management is hands-on: eager to help employees solve any problems and deal with any issues—but at the same time, don't micromanage. Give your employees enough space to take initiative, enough responsibility to feel they make a difference.

Remove codependency within the organization.

Cross-train all of your employees to perform each other's tasks, so when someone takes vacation time or is out sick, the company isn't crippled.

Create a title and job description for every single position within the company. And continually evaluate how well employees meet or exceed the standards on their job descriptions.

Be clear and specific about expectations.

Reward, acknowledge, and encourage employees in public; give "you can do better" messages in private. When a team contributes to a big success, honor the entire team, in public.

Avoid "silos"; have short weekly meetings to connect the loop between departments (for example: the accounting department depends on sales, so they should get together at least once a week and compare notes)

If you want to retain top-notch employees, give quarterly bonuses; a year is too long to wait.

Give employees their birthday off.

Celebrate birthdays once a month in the office...with cake (everyone loves cake!)

Your aim isn't to be superficial or phony, but to befriend your coworkers and create an environment where people think of their jobs as more than just a paycheck. Let them experience the consistent feeling that they're respected and appreciated. Show them that you truly encourage them to grow, learn, teach, and share their expertise. And build the camaraderie—the genuine team spirit based on trust and the sense that you're all in this together to create something bigger than any of you could develop by yourselves.

If you build successful relationships—both internally (with your employees) and externally (with your customers vendors, neighbors, and other stakeholders) —you'll increase that positive success energy in the workplace. Paperwork will flow efficiently, and all of your staff will honor the establishment and want to contribute to its success. And when that happens, the money flow will increase.

CHAPTER 18

I LOVE MONDAYS!

Takeaway Tools:

- **Positive Attitude.** Develop a positive attitude in everything you do. Mondays can be great days if you walk into them with a positive attitude.
- **Inspiring Others.** Let your attitude inspire those around you to join you in your journey toward success.
- **Share Your Success Mindset.** Whether you're facing an audit or a Monday, you have the power to create positive flow in your life. Organize your business for success today by harnessing all five days of the week.

Why do so many people hate Mondays? Studies show that productivity actually suffers on this day. But if you love what you do, shouldn't you look forward to going to work with the excitement of a whole fresh new week to make your mark on the world? Think of all the great projects on your Weekly Activities Planner, and how good you'll feel as you change them from to-do, to done.

Let's get rid of the Monday Blues, once and for all!

As a manager, I've made it my mission to change Monday's bad rap. In several of the companies I've worked for, I instituted an **I Love Monday** program that has worked miracles.

First, we look at why people resent Monday. Ask yourself these questions:

Why do most people dread Monday?

Why do production levels and efficiency suffer on Monday?

Why do so many people greet Monday with low energy and bad attitudes?

Why won't some people close deals on a Monday?

Why do people avoid going out on first dates on Monday?

There's one single, powerful, and simple answer to all these questions: People resent leaving behind a weekend of fun and freedom for the structure and work of the week day.

Monday usually means the end of play time. Too often, responsibility, routine, and even boredom dominate our work lives. The weekend mindset must become a weekday mindset—and, as the transition day, Monday takes the brunt of our complaints.

So the key is to change our mindset.

I love Mondays, because I think of them quite differently. To me, Monday is opportunity. It's a chance to accomplish something, to reach my goals, to make money, to learn, plan, and develop new ideas. Monday is exciting, because I get to be challenged, and to excel.

What would your business look like if you and your employees welcomed the first day of the week with excitement? What if you were enthusiastic about starting the week, rather than dreading it?

Instead of thinking of Mondays as the time when you forfeit your freedom, let Mondays introduce a fresh, new color into your world. Cultivate the attitude that you'll *gain* freedom on Monday, because you get to choose and implement your goals. You were on hold during the weekend, but now, you get to rev up your engines and steam toward success.

This simple attitude shift makes all the difference.

When I would call someone up on a typical Monday, I could hear their low energy and bad attitude. It came through in the tone of their voice—and in the grumbled answers to my cheerful "How are you?":

- "I'll be better on Thursday."
- "It's Monday, what do you expect?"
- "I wish it was still the weekend."
- "I would like to skip Monday and go straight to Tuesday."

That last response always made me laugh; *if we skipped Monday, then Tuesday would become the most unpopular day of the week. It's not the day. It's the attitude.*

It became my personal mission to defend Monday and show how it's the most important, fabulous day of the week—so I developed multiple ways to shift these bad attitudes:

Monday is your chance to change! Seize the opportunity to become a better partner…a more patient parent…a more productive employee…a better time manager…

Use Monday to do something that will make you feel great about your personal identity. It's a great day to accomplish something!

Convert stress into passion.

Enjoy the process of what you do. Embrace the actions that produce positive money flow.

Welcome responsibility. It's your chance to take charge!

You make things happen on Monday. Feel your power.

The more you take advantage of Mondays, the more freedom you have to enjoy your time off. In other words, the more successful and productive you are during the week, the more time you'll have for vacations and fun time on your days off.

Working productively for all five days of the workweek also generates more money to buy both the things you need and those you want—the frivolous fun things. If you're an entrepreneur or paid on commission, you can easily see the direct link between getting more done and being paid better. But even if you're an hourly or salaried worker, you'll find the payoff before too long—as your supervisors notice your good attitude and 20 percent greater productivity, and eventually offer you promotions and raises.

You get to solve problems every day of the week, and that's empowering.

Enjoy the moment. Don't carry yesterday's stress into today. Move forward and take advantage of fresh opportunities. It doesn't matter what day it is. You can make a difference right now.

If you'd like to know about changing your workplace to one where everyone loves Mondays, please visit www.moneyflowmastery.com/mondays, where you can buy a whole program about how to bring this extra joy into your work environment.

CHAPTER 19

IT'S THE ATTITUDE, DUDE

It's been fun to walk down memory lane with you. Hopefully, my journey inspires your own ladder of success. Before we leave the world of work and delve (in Part 3) into the keys to a happy and financially successful life, let's recap some of the core lessons of successful management.

Remember—it's all about *attitude*. With a positive attitude, your likelihood of success. is exponentially greater. Without it, why are you even in business?

P.N.P.

One of the most powerful tools I've developed to find and keep that positive attitude is P.N.P.: Passion, Negotiations, and Possibilities

Passion

Passion converts tomorrow's dreams into today's reality. Passion motivates us to pro-actively befriend life's challenges and responsibilities, lifting our energy level and bringing out our best. This reduces our stress and encourages our successfully.

Negotiations

The most important negotiations are between you and your nature; learn not to *fight* with your nature, but to *negotiate* with it instead.

When we learn to negotiate with our nature, we gently but firmly expand our boundaries and possibilities, while build a successful relationship with the one person we cannot escape: ourselves. As we improve our relationship with ourselves, we gain the negotiating and listening skills—and the confidence—to develop great relationships with people: at work, at home and in every other part of our lives. We filter our behavior…make better choices…and ultimately, we live happier lives.

Possibilities

We live in a world of infinite possibility—and we have to remind ourselves of that, each and every day. Using our powerful technology tools, we have almost unlimited access to information and resources about almost anything in the world…even everything human beings know about the rest of the universe. And we can reach out, communicate, network, and support people in every corner of the world, using social forums such as Facebook, LinkedIn, Twitter, and Pinterest.

And that means whatever we can dream, we can work with others to achieve. With enough patience and time, we can learn any skill, become knowledgeable about any process. And we not only achieve our money success goals, we can work together to create a world where no one is hungry or homeless, the people of the world live in harmony, and war is a distant memory.

Think of the rest of this chapter as a longer list of **takeaway tools**:

Hire the right people. A no-brainer: If you're very careful to hire qualified, high energy, optimistic workers with great people skills, and you pay them according to their performance and job pay scale, you'll create a dream team.

Turn the wrong people into the right people. If you inherit (or accidentally hire) a bunch of surly, clueless employees, they'll bring you down unless you take immediate steps to change the culture, build morale and cooperation, and get them focused on the right priorities. This is harder than hiring happy, motivated people to begin with, but it can be done. Remember, even Mrs. Schechter could change, once she was shown a little kindness. The next several bullets give you the secret.

Appreciate the people you hire. Show your employees that you value them and their work. Give them extra bonuses and perks whenever possible. Let them participate in some decisions and suggestions; implement their ideas when you can, and acknowledge their value even when their suggestions won't work—never put your employees or their ideas down publicly. When they see that you appreciate them, they'll work even harder for you. Remember that they know conditions on the front lines of your business in ways that you don't; their insights can slash your costs and pump up your profits.

Respect and have patience. Always manage your people with respect and patience. Never belittle or bully employees. If they know you're on their side, they'll do their best to live up to your expectations.

Cross-train employees. Although this is a key strategy, too few businesses put it in place. Managers think they're too busy to cross-train employees. Unfortunately, when an employee gets sick or leaves unexpectedly, they lose much more time trying to fill the empty slot because no one knows exactly how the job works. Abraham Lincoln famously said, "Give me six hours to chop down a tree and I will spend the first four sharpening the axe." When your employees can perform each other's jobs, your axe is much sharper.

Holdshort weekly meetings. Long, boring meetings can waste time in a company—but short meetings are great for improving understanding and communication—especially between departments. Short meetings give departments the chance to pinpoint issues, troubleshoot, and create specific action steps.

Encourage staff to take days off. What?! Yes, that's what I said. Encourage your staff to take a few days off now and then to refuel. When your employees can stop and fill their emotional and physical tank several times a year, they'll bring that energy back to the workplace. Oh yes, and make sure you take time off yourself, too.

Stop controlling. Your business will suffocate if you micromanage every aspect of it. Motivate your employees to take the initiative, and then publicly acknowledge their accomplishments. They'll not only take more pride in their work—they'll become more engaged and take even more initiative.

Create a happy environment. Design a workplace that people are eager to come to every day. Liven up the environment with music…attractive decorations…and good, healthy food to fuel their creativity. Remove clutter with a yearly cleanup; tossing out the junk saves money and space while improving the work environment. If the workplace is pleasing, your employees will actually want to be there.

Stick with the winners. Surround yourself with people who are energetic, healthy, and positive; their energy and positive vibes will rub off on you—both in business and in your personal life.

Provide opportunities for exercise. Physical health of employees is a significant factor in the health of a business. Put in some fitness equipment or offer your employees discounted memberships to nearby health clubs. Incent them to exercise, and watch productivity and morale rise (while health insurance costs shrink).

Make space for community involvement. If your employees' passions lead them into community service or betterment projects, facilitate that involvement (within some screens for compatibility of the project with your company's values and mission). Even let them set aside some work time for these projects. Companies that let their employees do service projects on company time see a huge boost in motivation and productivity, plus some significant PR in the community. Everyone, including your employees, wants to feel their actions make the world better.

Finally, remember that attitude starts with you. If you have a good attitude, almost everyone around you will tap into it. But a crummy attitude negatively affects everyone you interact with. What kind of vibe do you want to put out there? It's all in the attitude, dude!

(For more on this, read *Winning Without Intimidation* by Bob Burg, and *The Power of Nice* by Linda Kaplan Thaler.)

PART III

The Friends-with-Money Lifestyle

In this final part of the book, you'll learn to integrate money consciousness with other success drivers in your life. After all, there's no point in being wealthy if you're deeply unhappy—yet far too many people have plenty of money, but too little joy.

Living a happy and fulfilling life is not dependent on money (although money certainly makes it easier). True happiness depends on much deeper tenets like living well, knowing your values, and understanding that you make a difference to others. You'll be amazed at what happens when these values begin to permeate your entire day-to-day lifestyle!

The remaining chapters will help you build a smooth and integrated life of joy, even before you achieve your wealth goals. And then you can build on that lifestyle, as your finances continue to improve.

CHAPTER 20

You are creative—
life is awesome

Takeaway Tools:

- **Connection.** Creativity connects your contentment at home with your success at work.
- **Friendships.** Friendships and social occasions matter. They will deepen your understanding of others and improve your working and personal relationships.
- **Hobbies and passions.** Your creativity may inspire a new hobby or two. Enjoy it! It may become a passion.
- **Pamper yourself.** It's not only okay, but actually necessary to pamper yourself. Find healthy ways to recharge.

Do you consider yourself to be creative? Or are you one of those people who think creative types are weird or flaky?

In truth, we all have a creative side—and nurturing it will not only reduce your stress, but probably also make you more successful in your money quest.

So what kind of ROI (return on investment) will you achieve when you nurture your creative side? For starters, tremendous inner satisfaction, deep calm, and the wonderful ability to face challenges with equanimity—because your creativity will free you up to anticipate and bypass many problems, and solve many of the rest.

Creativity is also a great tool for business. Top CEOs are always looking to hire people with traits like imagination, innovation, originality, and ingenuity. Guess what—these are all synonyms for creativity.

Nurturing your creativity refuels your energy level; it opens your mind and heart to enjoying life much more deeply. To put it another way, creativity connects business success with personal success: If your creativity lets you open yourself up in all areas of your life, you're free to soar.

Creativity gives us a pause between responsibilities. It eases the tension and gives us just a little time to breathe, because it's open-ended. Instead of a regimented chore, it's a chance to explore something new. Creativity also gets us out of a jam. Nearly all human progress stems from creativity—as problems lead to new technologies and approaches that solve them. Imagine how dismal a world we would live in without the creative genius of Da Vinci (air travel and the Mona Lisa), Edison (inventor of electric lights, recorded music, and hundreds of other practical tools), Thomas Jefferson (the copy machine—and modern democracy), or Margaret Knight (an instant-stop mechanism that saved lives and limbs of countless factory workers, as well as the square paper grocery bag, among many other inventions). And of course, creativity gives us the great art and music and dance and writing that reminds us why life is worth living.

Hopefully, I've convinced you to open yourself to your own creativity. Now, how should you develop it? It's completely up to you—just make sure it's fun. What do you really enjoy—what ignites a spark in you? Music? Art? Dancing? Carpentry? Writing? Computers? Creating or solving puzzles? Communicating with animals? Making films or videos? Fixing cars? Improving a food crop? Flower arranging? Researching the secrets of particle physics? Finding thrift-shop clothes that make you look and feel like a million bucks? Those are just a few ideas among infinite possibilities; just let your mind create.

Give yourself permission to wonder and think about something new, to enjoy and experience the senses: sight, smell, touch, sound, and taste. Here's another great thing: You don't even have to be good at it! Just enjoy the process of creating. But don't be surprised if you discover that a creative hobby becomes a passion in your life, when you give it room to grow.

My own creative side opens up when I cook. I love combining rich flavors in dishes and smelling the aroma of a pot of soup simmering on the stove, and I love preparing and sharing meals. I've already mentioned the many business relationships that became lifelong friendships—and those friendships deepened my passions both for my job and for cultivating relationships with people around me. That wonderful gift was often strengthened through cooking. Once I've prepared a delicious meal for coworkers or friends, our bond deepens. We connect more deeply when we relax and break bread together.

Cultivating your creativity has one other huge advantage: you learn how to LET GO. When you create, you live in the moment. You can slough off yesterday's heartaches and disappointments; you may even realize that those setbacks just gave you a glimpse of what you don't want in your life. Drop them. Let go.

Through the lens of creativity, tomorrow is just as much an illusion as yesterday. You can plan for it, but it won't become a reality until you experience it and live it. So don't worry too much about the future, either. Let it go. Create. Stay in the moment.

Learning how to let go is one of the best tools I've gained in life. When I can reduce my emotional *and* physical clutter, I'm ready to move forward and embrace every event and every person who comes into my life; because I know that each experience is a necessary piece of my puzzle.

When I use my creativity and stay in the present, I see clearly how well this life fits me: I'm right where I'm supposed to be.

Your experiences and your passions will be different than mine; there's no one-size-fits-all approach to this. You have to find your own path, and nurturing your creativity will help you do that. Eventually, you'll discover that your own life fits you as well as mine fits me—and the sooner you begin to let go of what you can't control, the sooner you'll reach that point—and the happier you'll be. The clock is ticking forward whether you like it or not. So flow with it—become fully engaged in each and every moment.

Finally, use your creativity to honor yourself. Explore healthy ways to pamper yourself: Enjoy a hike through the woods; get a massage; go to a concert; meditate; take a yoga class; go to a baseball game; stroll through an art museum; take a nap on a Saturday afternoon; play a game with your children or grandchildren. All of these things not only feel good, they recharge you, help you let go, and release your mind to create new and exciting ideas. Be good to yourself! You deserve it.

Enjoy your creative side and consciously build this very useful tool that will help you flow easily along life's journey. Your creativity will lead you into a truly awesome life.

CHAPTER 21

Money principles in your personal and business life

Takeaway Tools:

- **Spend thoughtfully.** Be thoughtful about when, why, and where it makes sense to spend money. Shop for the best price and the highest quality. Conserve electricity, heat, water, paper, supplies, etc. Only buy what you need (keep the self-pampering to a minimum)—but when you need it, buy it.
- **Invest carefully.** Plan for when, why, and where you'll invest your money. Learn how to tell a wise investment from a foolish one.
- **Give joyously.** Recognize the importance of giving to charities and doing good deeds for others; your heart will be much lighter. Use your skills to help friends and family who are in need.
- **Accept graciously.** If you're the one who could use some extra help, and someone offers out of good motives, accept with gratitude.
- **Research thoroughly.** Learn every aspect of your personal and business finances and apply your money principles. Understand financing, credit terms, payroll, and debt. Pay your employees on time every time, and rid yourself of debt as soon as possible.

I love this chapter, because it gently reminds of the moments in my life when I let irrational emotions win, and I spent money unwisely. Boy, did I pay the price later!

Shopping is an emotional event. When we feel good about ourselves on the inside, we shop wisely—and not only is the shopping itself enjoyable, but we also feel good about what we bought, for a long time. But too often, when we get overwhelmed, we shop to make ourselves feel better momentarily ("shop therapy"). Unfortunately, this turns shopping into a nasty addiction. Just like a drug addict or an alcoholic, we get the craving, buy things we don't need, feel excited for a few minutes or maybe even a few days, wreck our finances and sometimes our personal lives—and then have to somehow swim back to shore from an ocean of guilt. And that's the opposite of fun.

Just as in the business world, you spell-check every important letter or email, train yourself to do a quick "shopping check" before you go out there and spend money. Take a few minutes to breathe if you feel an impulse-buying spree coming on. Connect the common sense/logical side of your brain with your emotional/heart side. Are they in sync? If not, put that credit card back in your wallet!

Money is like food. Portion, priority, and preparation are vital—and these are learnable skills. We must practice building *and* maintaining a healthy relationship with money. To develop healthy principles of money flow in our personal lives, we must treat money with respect. If we overspend on frivolous items that bring little or no real joy, we lose that respect.

Material things can bring a certain temporary thrill, but it only lasts a short while. "Toys" and fine things are tangible ways to show off; they feed the ego, but not the soul. They aren't deep or lasting—and just as I lost my dream home, my savings, and my not-yet-open restaurant in the earthquake, they can be yanked out from under you at any time.

I know several very wealthy people, and I'm happy for their success. They barely blink when they purchase a $400 pair of shoes; their bank accounts are bulging. But when personal challenges hit them, they hurt just like anybody else. That $400 pair of shoes may fit their feet, but it does nothing to soothe their heart in troubled times. Rich, "comfortable," or poor alike, every one of us has to work through those kinds of issues with the help of a deeper source.

Don't get me wrong—it's great to live an abundant life. Just don't get suckered into focusing on things that seem important but are ultimately much less important. If you focus on achieving material wealth and buying lots of luxuries, you may achieve that goal but create a shallow and meaningless life; it's not the way to find your true purpose.

A better goal is to have a wonderful money flow as part of a wonderful life. A healthy bank account is not an end in itself, but opens up exciting opportunities for you and frees you from fear of financial hardship. But no matter how much money you have, three things are always true:

Wherever you go, you cannot escape yourself.

You cannot control every situation and event in your life.

Because you're only human, you'll make mistakes. Everyone does.

Here's another one of my mistakes: a whopper:

So how can you maintain a positive relationship with money *and* live a great life? Start on the inside with these four emotional principles:

Accept who you are—befriend yourself.

When challenges arise, be proactive rather than reactive. Learn from mistakes and troubled times. Instead of letting yourself get tangled up in the problem, make a plan to get out of the muck and move forward.

Stop judging yourself and others; know that you are doing the best you can at that moment, with the skills and information you have right now (as is everyone else). It will free your spirit.

Remember that money can never be the real goal, because money is only a tool—one among many—to meet other needs and desires. Money is only meaningful for what it can buy. A stack of greenbacks in your drawer or a lot of digits in your bank account have no intrinsic value; their value is in what you can exchange them for. Many times, you'll be able to attract the solutions to your needs and the fulfillment of your desires without buying them—just as Mitchell gave me all the furniture I needed and Porsche gave me a beautiful new car.

Yes, money is your friend—but it's only one of many friends in your life. Your friendship with money will grow and thrive when you're guided by stronger principles. When you spend money wisely, you improve the money flow all around you. When you invest money wisely, you also nourish your relationship with money. And don't forget to give money freely, too. Your charitable contribution could make a huge difference in the life of someone in need—and that will infuse you with a far deeper and longer-lasting joy than the transient thrill of frivolous spending.

Money Principles in Business

In business and in your personal life, the same principles apply. Just as in your personal life, money principles in your business stem from your core values and your inner strength. Portion, priority, passion, and practice are just as important in business as they are in your personal life. Cultivate firm values for your company, and the money flow will follow. If your business is built on the solid principles I've shared throughout this book, your business will grow, rooted in a firm foundation.

As business owners, we need to be smart with our money. Making money your friend isn't just a nice idea—it's an essential skill for a successful business. We must learn when spending money will boost productivity and improve our employees' quality of life—and when overspending will hurt our business and our employees, causing layoffs or pay cuts. As we practice the principles we've learned, we get smarter about which purchases are essential and which ones are not, where we can save money, and where we should spend it.

CHAPTER 22

The power of no

Takeaway Tools:

- **Respect NO.** It's not such a bad word. Sometimes it will lead you in a better direction.
- **Find the Newly Opened Doors.** When certain possibilities are closed off, others open up. If I had married Hugo, I never would have seen the world. If I'd stayed with any of my early employers, I would not have a life as a writer and speaker today. When the road you think you want is blocked, look for a different road.

Both in business and in our personal lives, the word NO frequently challenges our ideas of success.

Some examples: When you encounter a NO, immediately disconnect your emotions so you can think clearly. Never take rejection personally; it's almost never really about you. Focus on steps to move around roadblock such as:

NO, you couldn't attend your first-choice university

NO, they didn't hire you for the job

NO, someone else put in a better offer on that house

NO, you loved someone who didn't love you back

NO, said the doctor when you made a wrong guess to diagnose your own illness

NO, screamed your child, spouse, parent, or other family member

NO as you tried to pursue an investment opportunity

NO to the credit card you applied for

What did you do when you were faced with rejection? How did you react? Responding correctly to those challenges is another key to success.

If I could turn every NO I've received in my life into a diamond, I'd be enormously wealthy. Hearing the word NO is part of life. We all experience it hundreds of times. So will you let that tiny little word defeat you? Of course not!

When you hear the word NO, let go of the unhappy feelings that understandably rush up. Other possibilities are all around you; this NO might open up a much better opportunity. Shift your thinking to replace your temporary disappointment with hope—a massively powerful tool to achieve happiness and success.

Several of the times I've heard the word NO—even some really huge, depressing ones—turned out to enable my greatest successes. Of course, I was devastated when they happened—but I realized years later that those NOs actually pointed me toward a much more positive life flow.

Let me tell you about one very heartbreaking NO that turned out terrific.

When I was seventeen, I went with my two best friends to a Chanukah party at a club in Ramat Gan, about an hour away from Tel Aviv. On that rainy December night, Rivka, Dalia, and I headed off to the bus stop for our grown-up adventure, promising to be home by 11:00 p.m. This party was an open house strictly for teenagers, with a few soldiers as chaperones. The three of us, all inexperienced, were so excited.

I didn't exactly have my party dress on, though. My mother had picked out frumpy clothes: a conservative black-and-white checkered pleated skirt, white sweater, black boots, and a gray coat with matching purse. From a distance, I looked like a conservative older woman—but up close it was obvious that I was a shy, young girl. I was still an introvert, and my girlfriends often teased me about my shyness.

We purchased our tickets and entered the hall, sitting down at one of the round tables. With wide eyes, we gaped at the festive tables laden with peanuts, cookies, hummus and pita bread, pickles, olives, oranges, and a cup of juice at every place.

The band played, "I Put a Spell on You," and I felt my heart racing. Love was in the air—I could feel it. Then I spotted a gorgeous young man standing behind the band. He was one of the organizers and therefore older, but I was captivated by him. I told my girlfriends that before the night was over, I would dance with him.

"What do you mean?" Rivka and Dalia laughed. "He won't even notice someone like you, with your old-fashioned hairstyle and conservative clothes."

But I cast my magic spell over him, and fifteen minutes before we had to leave, he walked over and asked me to dance. My girlfriends couldn't believe their eyes! Hugo was twenty-two, in his first year at the university, and he had served in the army for three years. And like me, he was an only child from Romania.

Hugo and I fell in love. We started dating, and to this day I still remember his passionate kisses and how wonderful I felt when he held me in his arms. Hugo loved the theatre, movies, music, and good books—but he had no interest in travel, foreign languages, international food, or socializing. I wanted us to be perfect together, but we had very different passions. Hugo wanted to stay in the country and go into politics. I dreamed of seeing the world.

It didn't matter. I was in love, and I would have followed him anywhere.

But Hugo wasn't willing to make a commitment until he reached the age of twenty-six. That's when my mother put her foot down. She said NO—in a loud, resounding voice—and I was devastated. Mom could see that we were not a good match, and she told me I could no longer date him.

Of course, I was devastated. At the time, I couldn't understand why my mother would say NO. Years later, I realized the breakup was the very best thing for me. I would have been so unhappy living in one place and never seeing the world! Traveling brings me much joy, and I can't imagine what my life would be like without the fascinating people I've met everywhere I go.

Over time, NO evolved into a worldly YES. I thank my mom for having the courage to say NO when I could not.

Whether you're hearing YES or NO, money is still your friend and ally. Your relationship with money must be respected and cultivated at all times. And NO still means NO, whether it's your mother or your boss saying it.

Sometimes, you might deliver the word NO to someone else. Just like that spell check on your computer, consider a "think check" before you say no to someone. It's a powerful little word, and hard to take back.

Create a solid set of values, and live by them. Then the word NO will not devastate you, but encourage you to look for better options and choose a happier, more fulfilling life.

CHAPTER 23

Don't be a slave to time

Takeaway Tools:

- **Which side is time on?** Like money, time can be your friend or your enemy.
- **Enjoy the courtship of time.** Use the Eight A's Time Solution Formula as a courtship: a way to romance time and make it your friend and companion.

Time can be your best ally—or your worst roadblock. And to create a successful money flow, you must understand how to work with time. We'll spend the next few chapters exploring that relationship.

Too often, we either become a slave to the clock—or we let someone or something else steal our precious time. In these chapters, you'll begin to recognize—and then overcome—the thieves that steal our time. We know who they are and how they operate. Now we need tools to arrest them! The Eight A's Time Solution Formula is the first such tool.

The Eight A's Time Solution Formula

The only way to deal with a problem or issue that can't be ignored is to solve it—and how we solve either increases or decreases the problem's impact on our time.

The Eight A's Time Solution Formula combines action, analysis, and reflection into eight effective techniques to arrest time thieves; some work best in certain situations, others work better at different times. To help you remember them, all of them begin with "A." Use these techniques to start to change the blueprint of your day. You'll arrest the time thieves and gain hours in your day every time you apply any of the Eight A's. Feel free to customize them to defeat your own particular time thieves.

Acknowledge how you feel about the theft of your time. Don't fight your feelings; they're part of you. Acknowledge them in order to understand why you surrender to those time thieves.

Analyze and understand the issues. Your thoughts are powerful; let them lead you.

Accept the challenge and face it with a new perspective. Fresh thinking and a new attitude go a long way toward finding solutions.

Act preemptively to control the situation—taking small proactive steps. Act, don't react; you're in charge of your destiny. Being proactive will shift your thinking.

Address issues you can control right now—but recognize the ones you can't affect. Some will work themselves out eventually, and others may not even be worth your time.

Admire others for their abilities—and figure out how to add those abilities to your own repertoire. Seek support and guidance for issues that you cannot solve alone.

Attend to your energy level. Don't let it be absorbed by time thieves!

Allow space and be patient. Enjoy the process! Don't dwell on how quickly you'll get from point A to point B; that's much less important than developing and implementing strategies to stop your time thieves.

CHAPTER 24

Arrest the time thieves!

Takeaway Tools:

- **Identify and banish the time thieves.** Once you know what's stealing your time, kick those things out of your life.
- **Be gradual—or be overwhelmed.** Don't expect to unlearn a lifetime of bad habits immediately. reward yourself when you interrupt the bad patterns, but don't beat yourself up if you slip back every now and then. Like anything else, it gets easier with practice.

Tricky time thieves hide among the necessary and important activities. Wearing numerous disguises, they infiltrate our noble pursuits and dreams of living good and rewarding lives.

Two main keys will help you arrest the time thieves:

- Moderation
- Common Sense

That's all you need when you're ready to stop being a slave to time and start kicking the time thieves out of your life!

Let's look at a few of those sneaky disguises:

Relationships

Relationships should be nourishing to both participants. But the wrong relationships—or wrong approaches to the right relationships—steal your time. When you dwell on them in counterproductive ways, they sap your energy.

So do your part to keep relationships healthy. Avoid all the negativity that tries to poke its ugly head up—from crowding the other person to fixating on what's lacking in the relationship. Negativity in relationships doesn't just steal your time; it can damage those relationships. When you find yourself in these situations, take a step back and focus your attention on something else.

This doesn't mean that you suppress conflict! Far from it—that's a sure way to destroy a relationship. Rather, when you do have a conflict, you work it out in ways that promote both of your goals and both of your self-esteem. Instead of making personal attacks, work together to identify and solve the real problem. As an example, instead of dumping a bucket of negativity on the other person with a phrase like "what a stupid idea," respond with something like, "That's a very creative approach, but I have some concerns about it [list them]. Can we think together about how to solve them?"

Health

Oddly enough, too much attention to health concerns can steal your time—especially if you focus on what's wrong and not on how to get healthy. Did you know that when you react to every perceived ache and pain, you can actually damage your health? It's true! The universe has a way of enhancing the things we focus on. So when you focus on pain, your body begins to treat the pain as its natural state. And this steals valuable time from working and improving on your overall health status.

Remember the moderation key. Acknowledge your feelings about your health concerns and take positive steps to improve your condition. But keep in mind that some things are not in your control, and others simply aren't very important in the big picture. Be proactive. Focus on the concerns you can most easily affect—like eating well and getting enough exercise.

Nineteenth century American humorist and lecturer Josh Billings said, "There's lots of people in this world who spend so much time watching their health that they haven't the time to enjoy it." Spend your time achieving health, not watching it slip away.

Fighting Our Nature

Trying to change our basic nature is difficult at best, and struggling against it is a time thief. True, you can't easily change who you are. But you *can* change what you do, and that almost always changes how you think and feel. First, determine what you can realistically change and accept what you cannot. Apply the changes in baby steps, and be enthusiastic about the changes as they progress. Changing what you do in achievable ways will bring new opportunities that will enrich your life.

Here's a simple "mantra" to keep you on the improvement path: "Stop trying to fight your nature; negotiate with it instead."

Multitasking

A great American proverb says, "If you can't ride two horses at once, you shouldn't be in the circus." In our ever-more-complex world, we often need to multitask—but multitasking, too, can become a time thief. Often, as we try to do more and more, we actually accomplish less and less. Multitasking works when you can properly balance all the tasks. But unless you reach that balance, some or all of them get shortchanged.

Some of us aren't very good at multitasking; we spread ourselves too thin and wear ourselves out. We have to recognize when we have too much on our plate. Saying no is often the fastest and easiest way to recapture lost time and move that pesky time thief on down the road. Seek help when you feel overwhelmed, but don't be shy about helping others when you can.

Perfectionism

As efficiency expert W. Edwards Deming famously said, "The perfect is the enemy of the good."

We only need to be perfect in a few of the things we do. If you're doing heart surgery, piloting an airliner, or doing something else where lives depend on your flawlessness, strive to be perfect (and put in the many hours of practice and instruction you'll need to sharpen your skill to a diamond point). But for most tasks, perfectionism is just another time thief. While it's important to do your best, it's even more important to recognize when the cost of doing more—in money, time, or stress—exceeds its value. Acknowledge and understand your feelings when perfectionism is stealing your time. Then focus your attention on something else. Use your common sense to decide what really needs to be perfect and what is good enough. Most things only need to be good enough!

Worry and Fear

Replace worry and fear with positive action—and gain back large chunks of time! A proactive approach goes a long way toward easing the underlying concern. Acknowledge and accept your fears; the calmer you are, the better you'll handle your real issues .

Remember: most of the things you worry about or fear never come to pass. Focus instead on more productive uses of your time, knowing that time and a positive approach will resolve many issues.

Anger

Even more than worry, anger is a particularly cancerous time thief—so, as with worry, learn to replace time stolen by anger with positive action. If something's wrong in the world, organize a campaign to rectify it. If something's wrong in a relationship, have a nonjudgmental heart-to-heart talk with the person you're angry with—and if he or she responds in anger, learn and use strategies to validate their concerns while defusing their hostility. Worry and anger are learned behaviors, and you can model better ones. When you focus on how you can make the world, your neighborhood, or even your home a happier place, you prevent anger from stealing your time. However, if anger is a constant time thief in your life—or if your safety is endangered by someone else's anger—seek help.

Blame and Judgment

Blaming or judging others never solves anything. Shift your thinking in this area, and examine the underlying issues that foster your defensiveness. Instead of blaming someone else—take personal responsibility to solve the problem (on your own, or with help from others).

Envy

Acknowledge and accept your feelings, and gain perspective. There's no point in dwelling on other people getting the things you think you deserve. Rather, understand how they achieved this—and how you can, too.

Wasting Time

You can never get back a wasted hour. Be mindful of how you spend your time and what it costs you to waste it. Set up systems to stay efficient—so, for example, you don't waste time looking for something, because you've put it right where it belongs and you know exactly where it is. Learn to "hit the ground running" when you start a new task or project, so you don't fritter away the time in a long warm up.

Do build in time to decompress, though. Time you spend walking in the woods, meditating, reading a good book, cooking a nice meal, or listening to a beautiful piece of music is not wasted; it's essential!

Important Note about These Unproductive Habits

You're talking about changing a lifetime of poor habits; don't expect to learn the new strategies instantly and make them a part of your core personality right away. It took you and the people around you years to learn these negative thinking and negative behaviors; replacing them with positive ones will also take time. But you can start right away.

Notice when you get caught up in your old, unproductive habits. Then, shift your thinking and your behavior; dump those useless habits and spend your time on more productive activities. Every time you stop a negative thought, speech, or action pattern, you've won a little victory.

Reclaim Your Time

The Eight A's Time Solution Formula helps you minimize the unproductive behaviors that steal huge amounts of our time and should have no place in our lives. Immediately, you'll start to reduce their power over you; eventually, you'll eliminate them from your life. Just knowing that these behaviors are time thieves—and approaching them with determination and patience—go a long way to reducing their impact on your life.

The Eight A's Time Solution Formula lets you take control of your time, become more productive, lower your stress, and have more fun. Every time you apply the formula, you're arresting another sneaky time thief.

Because success with the formula requires feedback, the next tool for confronting and defeating the time thieves lets you keep track of how much the time thieves have stolen from you. More importantly, you also track the time you recapture. Once you've been using the chart below for a few weeks, you'll easily spot the improvement. You'll rapidly gain more and more control of your time. Congratulations—you're no longer a slave to time and no longer a victim of the time thieves.

Week:	S	M	T	W	T	F		
				Stolen Time				
Time Thieves								
Relationships								
Health								
Fighting our nature								
Multitasking								
Perfectionism								
Worry								
Anger								
Fear								
Blame & Judgment								
Jealousy								
Unproductive Habits								
Wasting Time								
Total Lost Hours								
				Recovered Time				
Additional Activities								
Total Recovered Hours								
				Time Balance				
Net Lost or Recovered Hours								
				Notes				

CHAPTER 25

Taming the email tiger

Takeaway Tools

- With a good system in place, email can turn from a curse back into a blessing.
- Keep to a schedule for managing email.
- When you can answer something completely, do. When you can't, keep the other person informed.
- Move messages out of your inbox and into folders; keep your inbox as fresh and clean as possible.

Managing Your Email

Not so long ago, when we sent someone a message, we had to type it, proofread it, re-type if it needed revisions, fold the paper into an envelope, place the envelope in the mailbox—and then wait days or even weeks for a response. If we wanted to include others or keep a reference copy for ourselves, we had to go use a copy machine—and before that, carbon paper. Now, we quickly address and type a message, add any number of recipients, spell-check it, read it over quickly, click SEND, and expect a response within hours—at the latest. We send pictures and documents by email. We often prefer email to talking on the telephone or even to walking across the hall to speak with a co-worker, because email documents our intent and our agreements. Used correctly, email is an indispensable productivity tool and time-saver.

But for too many people, email is a time thief. Because it enables instant and constant communication, email has dramatically increased the volume of messages. For many people, email is now a time trap and an impediment to productivity.

Do you receive more than 10 emails a day?

Do you get bogged down with junk email?

Do you sometimes get irritated by email?

Does it feel like email is in control of you?

Do you have hundreds or even thousands of emails in your inbox?

Are you unhappy with the results of your emailing efforts?

Each "yes" means you need a better way to handle email. Here's my system to deal with email effectively and efficiently, create time for other things, increase your productivity, and improve your relationships. Like all my other advice, choose what parts are useful for you, with your own patterns and situation.

Business Email

Effective business email management requires that you:

- Check your inbox regularly—But NOT compulsively.
- Process your email in a timely manner.
- Keep your inbox clean.

Email arrives all day long, even when you're asleep. Some messages need a pretty quick answer; others can wait, or don't even need a response. People who send you business email expect a quick or at least timely response. Procrastinating can hurt your career and damage your business relationships.

Set several specific points in your day to check your email. For instance, you might check email after you've completed one non-email project in the morning, when you return after lunch, and an hour before you go home. Give the important email time it requires—but set limits on it. For instance, you could set a timer for 30, 45, or 60 minutes—and when it rings, finish the email you're writing if it's quick, save it as a draft if it's more involved, and go back to the other things you choose to accomplish that day.

Speaking of ringing—turn OFF the notification sound that tells you there's new mail. All it does is drive you crazy wondering what came in, and distract you from your real work. You know that mail is pouring in all day, but that doesn't mean you have to drop what you're doing to deal with it, any more than you'd drop your work project due today anytime a co-worker saunters by and wants to chat.

More Tips

Delete the junk mail. You can reduce the junk by adjusting your junk mail filter, but be careful not to set it so high that you filter out important email. In most cases, it only takes a few moments to just delete the junk mail. But if you work in areas like marketing or finance, you can't just flush the junk unread, because a lot of important mail will get lost there. Open your junk folder, select all, deselect the few important ones, and then trash the selected ones and move the others to your inbox.

Sort the messages in your inbox to suit your needs at that precise moment. You can usually sort by date, subject, sender, priority, attachments, and so on. If a conversation thread is not relevant to you, sort by subject and trash all the emails with that subject line, all at once.

Process Your Email in a Timely Manner

Delete everything unread that you don't need to read, or that doesn't interest you, or that invites you to something you can't attend.

Reply to all of the incoming messages that you can completely answer with only the information you already have at your fingertips.

For emails that need a more involved response, acknowledge the message and indicate when you expect to reply. If you think that might take a while, explain why. For instance, you might need to:

- Get more information or input.
- Complete an activity before you can report on it.
- Move those messages into clearly named folders. Tag the folders by priority.
- Quickly scan and file emails that contain information you need to know, but don't need to respond to, especially if you're just being copied on an email aimed at someone else.
- Delete any email you don't need to refer to again, or any email with low enough priority that you haven't read it in a week.
- Get help from your supervisor and/or co-workers if you get bogged down responding to an email. Spinning your wheels is a time killer.
- Keep your inbox clean.

Even after you've responded, you'll want to keep a lot of email. But that doesn't mean the messages have to stay in your inbox! As soon as you've dealt with an email, move it to its appropriate folder.

Decide on a principle of organization that makes sense for you and for your job. A few examples:

If you work in sales, create a folder for each customer.

If you work in purchasing, create a folder for each vendor.

If you work in product development, create a folder for each project.

If your work spans several interest areas or disciplines, create a folder for each one.

When a category gets too crowded, create subfolders in each of the folders.

Archive the folders when they get too big, or every six months to a year. This will keep them smaller and easier to use, and you can always retrieve emails from the archives.

Of course, the more you can do to keep the quantity of incoming messages under control, the less of a burden email will be. Here are some ways to minimize the flood:

Encourage co-workers NOT to cc people who don't need to be in the loop for a particular issue.

Unsubscribe from any newsletter or discussion list that isn't adding value. If you read three to five issues of a newsletter or two weeks of a discussion list and it doesn't give you good information you can use, get rid of it. (Shel often sorts by sender and reads a bunch of newsletters from the same sender all at once—which makes it easy to determine if there's enough value to stay on the list.)

Use a separate email address (perhaps a Yahoo or Hotmail address) to sign up for anything on the web; if they sell your name to spammers, the junk will go to the low-priority address. Don't click banners or popups or follow any links claiming you've won something—unless it was a specific contest you remember entering—or pretending to need your help to transfer a large sum of money.

When you receive an email that needs a response but is ambiguous, ask very specifically for clarity, for instance, "I don't understand when you say..." or "I could interpret this in several ways—which did you mean?"

If you run a newsletter, use one of the respectable email services to send it out and to manage the subscriptions. You'll lose an enormous amount of productive time if you have to manually subscribe, unsubscribe, and change the addresses of your readers.

Write and Send Better Emails

Used correctly, email is a delightful and easy way to connect with loved ones, family members, friends, and neighbors—and an essential tool for keeping and maintaining both business and personal relationships. Now, a few tips to make others happier when they see your name in their inbox. Before you hit SEND:

- Always spell check.
- Always check the recipient(s), especially if you select names from your address book.
- Keep emails brief and to the point.
- Don't be part of the problem. Make sure you're not copying people unnecessarily...your instructions and questions are clear, brief, and to the point...you provide high-value content if you have a newsletter or participate in social media... and NEVER spam people...you include polite human touches like "great to see you at the Chamber mixer last night" or "hope your daughter is over her cold."
- Call when you can. It will create a more intimate connection.
- Email and ask: "When is a good time to call you? I have to share something amazing with you!"
- Email can stand for more than electronic mail; it can also mean ENJOY your mail.

Personal Email and Social Media

Personal email and social media—including correspondence over Facebook, LinkedIn, Twitter, Google+, and similar social networks—is just as important as business email, but should be simpler to manage. You can use any or all of the business email system to tame this smaller email "tiger cub." Just remember that there are no secrets over email or social media; any email you send or note you post could be passed around or even go public. A good rule: never post or send anything you would be ashamed of if your mother saw it on Page One of her newspaper.

Benefits of Using a System

Whether you choose my system or one that works for you, you'll experience lots of benefits when you systemize your email:

- Reduced stress
- More control and organization of your work
- Better relationships with email correspondents
- More time for other things
- Improved corporate reputation, growth, and revenue

CHAPTER 26

Time can be your friend

Takeaway Tools:

- **Cut.** Cut out the time thieves in your life.
- **Ignite.** Ignite your passions in your day-to-day life—at home and at work.
- **Find.** Find more time to do the things you love.
- **Delegate.** Delegate tasks you don't enjoy to people who actually like doing them.
- **Systemize.** Create a simple system to set your priorities and allocate time for every task or duty.

What's a section on communication doing in a chapter on time management? Actually, effective communication is an integral part of time management. When you communicate clearly in ways that empower others, you remove delay-causing "friction"; things go more smoothly and much faster, you can cross many more things off your tasks, and have that much more time for the next project. And when you set aside specific chunks of time to communicate, it doesn't swallow your whole day.

Just as you can create more money by wisely investing what you already have, you can also create more time. In the next few pages, I'll give you specific practical tools to maximize your time in five different areas:

- Following-up and feedback on communications
- Overcoming procrastination
- Ending micromanaging
- Getting through your personal do list
- Checking your behavior with a taboo list

Using these simple tools will provide you with a substantial return for a small investment of your time. You'll discover very strong connections among these six areas; mastering them strengthens your skill in controlling your work instead of letting your work control you. And as you gain that control, you may suddenly start to love your work—and your life.

Communicating Effectively

- Do you often forget or neglect to get back to people?
- Do people seem to avoid your calls?
- Is your staff unresponsive to you?
- Do you leave multiple messages before people get back to you?

Every "yes" is a sign that you could improve your communication skills.

Make better use of your time, improve your communications of all types, and greatly improve your follow-up and feedback. Here's my system for improving follow-up and feedback as part of generally improving communications skills and time management.

Ana's Communications Time Management System:

- Allocate the right amount of time for communications
- Understand the types of communications
- Build communications into your schedule
- Work through your schedule

Allocate the Right Time for Communications

Everyone needs to spend some work time every day communicating—but how much time and what types of communications depends on your daily tasks, the nature of your work and the culture of your company. Since it's important to build that time into your daily schedule, here are some ways you might allocate time for communications.

- A manager might choose this split:
  - Telephone: 0.5 hour
  - E-mail: 1 hour
  - Face-to-face: 2.5 hours
- A salesperson might divide the day this way:
  - Telephone: 2 hours
  - E-mail: 0.5 hour
  - Face-to-face: 4 hours
  - Written correspondence: 0.5 hour

- An attorney might set up this sort of day:
    - Telephone: 0.5 hour
    - E-mail: 0.5 hour
    - Face-to-face: 3 hours
    - Written correspondence: 1 hour

Regardless of how you distribute it over your day, be sure to build communications time into your schedule.

Immediate and Delayed Communication

Communications either happen immediately, or they don't. If you're communicating over the phone, Skype, or in person (with the obvious exceptions of voicemail and recorded presentations), the other person is right there, receiving information—and usually participating. Email and postal mail, on the other hand, happen in stages; you write, and then some time later, the other person answers. This distinction becomes important as you schedule your communications.

Build Communications into Your Schedule

Here's my method of building communications into your daily schedule:

- List all the people you need to communicate with during the day and the type of communication each requires. Also assign a priority to each communication. This should only take a few minutes.
- Schedule the face-to-face and telephone appointments, allocating enough time for each, starting with the highest-priority meetings. Call to confirm their availability and tell them the purpose and the expected duration. Adjust your schedule to accommodate them, as necessary.
- If you can't reach someone, leave a voicemail requesting an appointment. Specify the purpose, estimate the time you'll need, and suggest a preferred and an alternate time. Example: "Hi, Jack, it's Ana Weber-Haber. Could I get 15 minutes with you to go over the conference presentation? I've tentatively written you in for noon. 3 o'clock is also possible. Please call to confirm." Follow up your voicemails with email—but note that for same-day meetings, scheduling by phone makes a lot more sense, because your correspondent may not see the email in time.
- If you can't schedule a same-day meeting or call, schedule it for another day.
- Once you've scheduled your telephone and face-to-face meetings, allot time for e-mail and postal correspondence.

If possible, select low-demand times such as early or late, or when others are at lunch.

Work Through Your Schedule

Be flexible:

- Sometimes, people will need to reschedule at the last minute; use this "found time" for other productive activities—it's a gift to you.
- If an appointment runs long, determine if you have time to finish right then. If you don't, schedule a continuation.
- When you have to postpone or cancel, contact those people as soon as possible to explain and reschedule.

Following-up and Feedback

As business success tools, follow-up and feedback are second only to excellent staff; they're two of the most important tools in our communications tool kits—and we can learn to do them well! Beyond better meetings, these specific practices will directly improve your follow-up and feedback—and thus, your time management:

Follow-Up

Follow-up is the branch that really bears fruit. I divide it into three parts:

1. Focus on the material in the NOW: what steps do you need to take in order to move a project or a relationship forward?
2. Be mindful of priority: which things need to get done first?
3. Take action: organize and connect: who else needs to be doing what, how will they work in teams, and who's making sure the work gets done in time?

Consider the follow-up task as a stand-alone activity, separate from the emotions you may have around it. For instance, if you're feeling frustrated because a co-worker has not kept a promise to get something done, instead of belittling the co-worker out of your own frustration, work together to determine where the stuck place is and how to get around it. Often, it may not even be that person's fault, because he or she is waiting for someone farther up the line.

Follow-Up Folder

Enter required follow-ups (to emails, voicemails, meetings, and correspondence) on your action items list, and put the items in a separate follow-up folder.

- Jot down short notes to help focus each response in

appropriate and useful ways.

- Give priority to urgent or timely items. The right response at the wrong time is no better than the wrong response.

Feedback

It's natural for us to expect feedback and recognition—not out of ego, but through the desire to feel that we did something good as we contribute to the betterment of the society.

When you give feedback about their ideas, their work, and even their behavior, validate the people receiving it and assure them that they have your support. Although most of us are trained in childhood to dump a bucket of negative energy on those we disagree with, this not only doesn't move the agenda forward, it unnecessarily creates enemies, defensiveness, and resistance to improvement. Feedback should always be positive and constructive; take the time to learn the skill of framing things positively.

Like other kinds of communication, feedback can either be immediate (in the moment) or deferred (giving you time to compose your thoughts and ensure a positive tone). In addition to this difference, treat feedback about behavior issues differently from feedback about their ideas or the quality of their work.

Immediate Feedback

Because immediate feedback is reactive, given on the spot, it's doubly important to be positive and constructive—because once the words are out of your mouth, you can't take them back. Of course, you must be honest. But there's no need to be brutal or mean. Instead, express negative criticisms in positive and constructive terms. This is a learned skill, and gets better with practice.

1. *Ineffective*: "Your plan won't work because of X, Y, and Z."
2. *Effective*: "I think your plan is a good start, but have you considered X, Y and Z?" You might even offer to help refine the plan.

Deferred Feedback

Deferred feedback is given after the fact, allowing you time to think and reflect before offering it. This lets you be more nuanced and thoughtful, to find the merit in the idea, and also to see problems that might not be obvious on the first glance. Deferred feedback gives you plenty of time to cast any negative opinion you might have in constructive terms. However, with deferred feedback, you run the risk that you or the other person have forgotten the details of the incident, and the opportunity to improve may be diminished.

- *Ineffective*: "I've reviewed your plan, and I don't think it will work because you didn't address X, Y, and Z."

- *Effective*: "I reviewed your plan, and I like your thinking. I need to know how you plan to address X, Y and Z, which are my concerns as we think about implementing this." Again, you might even offer to work together.

Feedback on Behavior

Feedback about behavior should clearly convey your position without insulting the other person. Feedback regarding positive behavior should encourage more of that behavior. Feedback on negative behavior should never be personal; keep it about the behavior you want to change, not about the person who committed the act—and have negative conversations in private to avoid shaming or embarrassing the other person (though it may be useful to let others know that you *are* addressing the situation):

- *Ineffective*: "You did a lousy job explaining the situation to the customer. You were too concerned about yourself to understand their needs." Even though it pinpoints the problem, there is nothing positive about this feedback, and it is personal.
- *Effective*: "I liked that you addressed the competitive landscape, but I think you might have tried a different approach in explaining the situation to the customer. Customers are concerned about their needs and don't particularly care about your needs. I've found that your needs will be usually be met when you focus on satisfying the customer's needs." This feedback is positive and constructive—and accurate.

Benefits

As you learn to communicate more effectively, good things will start happening:

- By confirming times and topics of your meetings and telephone calls in advance, you'll allow the actual meeting or phone time to be much more focused and productive.
- You'll build great relationships with both internal and outside contacts—who will even start to seek you out and request your opinion.
- You'll bring in more business from new and existing customers.
- You'll bring positive energy to your work/organization, which will inspire your co-workers.

Positive attitude is crucial throughout the business environment, not just in feedback and follow-up. Pay close attention to this sequence:

- When you stay focused in the present time, you release the clutter around you and you do your best work.
- If you like what you do, you get results.
- When you get results, you gain more self-confidence and self-worth.
- When you produce results for others, you earn appreciation and rewards.
- You make the company money, and you increase your income.
- You feel good. You live well, and you enjoy the time spent working.

Postponement can be a virtue or a vice. It shows virtue—patience and good judgment—when you postpone for good cause:

- Postponing an important decision to wait for necessary information
- Postponing an expensive purchase until you have the savings or financing to cover it
- Postponing the start of a new project while new employees come up to speed
- Postponing disciplining your children as they reflect on the consequences of their actions

But postponing for no good reason is the vice of procrastination—and all it accomplishes is delay. Eventually, you still have to solve the problem, address the situation, or just get the project done; the only effective way is to actually do it!

Procrastination is an attitude. Some people procrastinate as a way of life. They postpone everything: work duties, personal chores, etc. Others procrastinate because they feel overwhelmed by the challenges and obstacles in their lives. Regardless of why people procrastinate, the result is always the same: things don't get done. Procrastination is a terrible time thief!

The Impact of Procrastination

The clutter of unfinished business fills our lives, impacting us emotionally and making it even more difficult to get things done. But procrastination doesn't just hurt the procrastinator; it starts a chain reaction that spreads its negative impact over an ever-widening area:

- Other peoples' schedules get pushed back as they wait for us.
- Some people give up on us and make other arrangements — robbing us of both current and future business.
- Our relationships with others suffer as they lose confidence

in our abilities.

Real Life Examples

- Wanting to get in shape, Judy decided to join a gym. But every day, she made new excuses about why she couldn't get there; she never did join. She could have improved her health, mental clarity and focus, appearance, and stress level. The only thing that stopped her was procrastination.
- Keith's house needed some upgrades. He made a plan but never acted on it, postponing again and again. Later, when he wanted to relocate for a great new job, he couldn't sell his rundown house at a price that would enable the move, and had to turn down the new position. His procrastination stymied his career.
- Larry received a large order from a steady customer. He committed to ship it in six weeks. But he waited a week to order materials that were out of stock, and then found out it would take another three weeks to receive them. Not wanting to deliver bad news, he didn't inform his customer. The shop was very busy when the shipment arrived, and because Larry procrastinated informing the shop manager, the job was scheduled in the order the materials were received. Only when the shipping date came and went did Larry finally share the situation with the customer—who, not surprisingly, placed his next order with a competitor. Larry's procrastination, first in ordering the materials, and then in informing the production manager and the customer, ended this profitable relationship when the customer lost confidence in Larry's ability to execute orders on time—and in his integrity.

Practical Steps to End Procrastination

Whether procrastination is an attitude or even a habit, you can take practical steps to end it:

- Every Monday, prepare a fresh action list for the week.
- Set your priorities and mark them right on the list.
- Adjust as needed during the week.
- Ask for help—from coworkers or even from outside sources—when needed.
- Resolve and cross off simple matters throughout the day, as

you have time between larger projects.

- Use clear and prompt communication to buy time when you don't have an answer or a clear response to a request, but don't procrastinate.
- Set a timeframe for each action item, based in your experience and common sense.
- Pro-act and return to your action list when you find yourself procrastinating.
- Clean up your list at the end of each day; start the next day with a fresh list.
- If you are responsible for others, conduct a brief meeting on Friday to check their action lists for the week just completed.
- Cross-train and help one another to accomplish as much as possible during the work day. A good and organized employee should almost never need to work overtime, except under extraordinary circumstances.

Procrastination is about attitude. When you catch yourself starting to procrastinate, say the word "act" or "accomplish" to yourself. With practice, your attitude will shift and you will find it easier to shift from procrastination to pro-acting. Occasional procrastinators usually find this helpful immediately. It may take a bit longer to impact full time procrastinators, but ultimately it will work for them too.

If you find yourself procrastinating because you get stuck on one of your action list items, put it down for a while and do something else on your action list. Your energy gets drained when you get blocked. Not only will doing something else on your list allow you to make productive use of your time, but it will also stimulate you—refueling your energy and giving your subconscious the chance to develop a fresh approach to the sticky problem when you do come back to it (maybe a few hours later, maybe the next day—not any later than that). The best way to take a break is to do something; if you do nothing, the time thieves have robbed you again!

The Benefits

When you stop procrastinating, you'll gain:

- Increased efficiency
- Faster progress in your career
- Improved business relationships
- More speed in closing deals
- More money
- Higher self-worth

- Respect from others
- More clarity
- Reduced stress
- Uplifted attitude at work
- Increased enjoyment from your work
- And of course, MORE TIME!

Quotes on Procrastination—an Age-Old Concern

Procrastination is such a time thief that many famous people have commented on it over the years.

Procrastination is the art of keeping up with yesterday. (Don Marquis – American writer, columnist, novelist, playwright and poet)

Middle age is the time when a man is always thinking that in a week or two he will feel as good as ever. (Don Marquis)

The leading rule for the lawyer, as for the man of every other calling, is diligence. Leave nothing for tomorrow which can be done today. (Abraham Lincoln)

How does a project get to be a year behind schedule? One day at a time. (Fred Brooks, The Mythical Man-Month: Essays on Software Engineering)

I don't wait for moods. You accomplish nothing if you do that. Your mind must know it has got to get down to work. (Pearl S. Buck)

In short, all these famous luminaries agree: Pro-act and do not procrastinate, you will gain freedom in time.

Ending Micromanaging

Few things keep us from achieving our potential more than obsessing over details—in our personal lives, and especially in business. Micromanaging keeps us from getting things done, steals tremendous amounts of our time, and wears us out! Ironically, the more little details we try to control, the less control we actually have.

As we gain more responsibility, we need to accomplish more—but that doesn't mean we need any more on our plates. Ask yourself:

Do you like to take care of everything yourself?

Do you think that you can do everything yourself?

Do you believe that only you can do things right?

Do you dislike asking others for help?

Do you believe that by doing it all yourself, you'll save money and time?

With every "yes," you accomplish less!

You can easily stop micromanaging. Once you understand the true cost of micromanaging, you'll be quite motivated to take effective action to end it.

The Cost of Micromanaging

Micromanaging takes one of two forms. Either we try to do everything by ourselves, or we constantly look over people's shoulders. In either case, micromanaging results in inefficiency, lost productivity, and lowered morale.

Things don't get done; they don't get done well, or they don't get done efficiently.

Other people's talents are wasted or misused; the business loses the value they could have contributed.

Resentment builds against the micromanager.

Remember: everyone does some things well, but no one, not even you, does everything well. If you need to get something down from the top of a tree, ask a squirrel, not a fish. If you're a fish trying to supervise a squirrel, asking the squirrel to become a better swimmer doesn't help either of you.

Why do we feel that we need to be in control of every process? Except when legal compliance requires a very specific procedure, our real objective is usually to get something done—not to control the way it gets done. To put it another way, we need to focus on *what gets done*, and **not** on *how it gets done*. But when we micromanage, the *what* gets lost in the *how*; things don't get done and our business suffers. We need to "grok" the consequences of micromanaging: the real costs in inefficiency, lost productivity, and crumbling morale.

Take Effective Action to End Micromanaging

Now that you understand how costly micromanaging really is, let's get rid of it! Start with this four-step method:

Understand your strengths and weaknesses

Connect with others

Let your organization organize

See the big picture

These actions work together. For example, your strengths provide the best results when you also connect with others in your organization to fully harness their unique strengths.

Understand Your Strengths and Weaknesses

What are you really good at, and what do you enjoy doing? Where those two intersect is where you want to spend the most time, because you can leverage these strengths and get far more done. These areas provide the greatest return for your time investments—while those where you have neither skill nor passion generate the least return.

Take an inventory of your responsibilities, and rank them by the intersection of skill and joy.

Now, assign yourself tasks that take advantage of your strengths—but only enough to fill your plate. Delegate assignments that play to your weaknesses to others whose strengths complement yours; the task will get done faster and better.

If you're not authorized to delegate, make sure your supervisor understands your strengths and weaknesses; a good manager will *want* to take advantage of your strengths. And if you're assigned a task in one of your weak areas, ask for help *before* you get bogged down.

Connect With Others

Most of what you do needs to get done—but you don't need to actually do all of it yourself. As you focus on what you do best and scale back the things you don't do well, you'll need other people to take those tasks. If you want others to pick up the slack, you need to connect with others. You can best understand their strengths and weaknesses when you have a good relationship with them. They'll shine when you showcase their strengths—and more will get done.

Let Your Organization Organize

Well-run companies are organized to focus on employees' skills and talents. If you make personnel decisions, assess each employee's strengths and weaknesses and match their responsibilities with their strengths. If, organizationally, you can't harness your strengths, work with your superiors to change that. Everyone will benefit.

See the Big Picture

Looking at the big picture helps you gain perspective. Some of what you think you need to do may be ultimately unimportant, and you could leave those pieces undone and still complete the job successfully. Prioritize what really needs to be done. Perfect is the enemy of good!

The Benefits

When you stop micromanaging, you will…

Gain a greater appreciation of the big picture, enabling you to make better strategic decisions.

Increase productivity.

Shine in the eyes of others who see you investing your best in the business

Make your co-workers look good as well, when they start harnessing—and being recognized for—their own strengths

You will enjoy better relationships with your co-workers, as you make take time to connect with them.

Attract more money and success.

Ana's Tips to Stop Micromanaging

Well-managed companies implement practices to minimize micromanaging and get the most from their employees. They…

Have a structure chart that shows everyone the big picture—each person's duties and responsibilities, from top to bottom.

Train new employees to excel in their positions.

Cross-train employees for better flexibility and to protect themselves when key employees leave the company—whether permanently or merely for vacation or illness.

Hold well-run, focused weekly meetings to go over their immediate agenda and allow everybody to understand what is expected from them—and, ideally, to boost morale and increase participation.

They confirm meetings a day ahead. This allows everybody to be better prepared for meetings, and also facilitates rescheduling when necessary—using everyone's time more efficiently.

Good leadership is the one intangible that every company needs. If you want to be a good leader…

Work-hands on with your employees and manage without resorting to fear tactics.

Connect with employees and get to know them as individuals.

Motivate your employees with positive rewards, targeted (if practical) to each employee's preferences. Happy employees will change the entire company's morale and improve overall effectiveness.

Respect each employee's professional and personal integrity.

Provide professional and growth opportunities for your employees.

Time spent wisely increases the bottom line!

Your Do Lists

While the portioning worksheets we looked at in Chapter 3 help you plan your monthly, weekly, and daily activities, your Do Lists provide a quick reference to help keep you on track as you go through your day. For each day, you'll want one list for business tasks, and another for other areas of your life. As with the earlier worksheets, I recommend downloading the templates from my website, **www.themoneyflow.com/worksheets,** so you can easily generate a fresh list every day, carry over not-done items without retyping, and instantly sort by any column.

Business Do Lists

A Business Do List should track the following information.

Order of priority

Vendor or client company

Task description (very brief)

Contact (name, phone, and if it's not already in your email program, email address)

Notes and reminders, which you can enter as you create the list, and also as you work through it

When customers require multiple tasks, make separate entries for each and sort them based on urgency, as in #s 4 and 5 in the example below.

#	Company	Task	Contact	Notes
1	LMN Company	Follow-up on manufacturing defects issues.	Larry, manufacturing manager. (333) 555-6789	They are investigating issues with their vendor. Will follow up again on Friday.
2	XYZ Company	Get updated requirements documents.	Joe Mendez, marketing manager (111) 555-2345	Called twice. Left voice mail asking him to call me.
3	XYZ Company	Set up planning meeting for next Tuesday.	Sharon Smith, project manager (111) 555-1234	Best time to call is 10:00.
4	ABC Inc.	Review ABC's requirements for quote.	Jerry Potts, communications manager (222) 555-1234	Unable to get all data. He will call me back with more info on Wednesday
5	ABC Inc.	Provide information for us to get on ABC's approved vendor list	Steve in accounting X432	Steve will email info to them tomorrow morning.
6	XYZ Company	Make travel plans for Tuesday meeting.	Rose @ Land & Sea Travel 621-3399	Try to get early morning flight.

Tips for Business Do Lists

Create a folder on your computer for Do Lists.

Make a new Do List every day and put the date right in the filename (such as "06-18-13 Do List")

Keep the list up on your computer screen, or a paper copy on your desk. Add notes as you go through it.

Carry over any tasks that didn't get done during the day.

Move Do Lists to a subfolder or archive every week or every month; don't delete them. It's often useful to refer back to them months or even years later.

Getting Through Your Personal Do Lists

Just as it does in business, your Personal Do List lets you easily keep track of both routine and occasional activities. A Personal Do List is organized around tasks, rather than customers or vendors. It tracks the task, contact people, and notes, but doesn't need the company field:

Task	Contact	Notes
Make dentist appointment	Dr. Samos, 555-2468	Appointment @ 10:30 on April 6
Invite friends to potluck dinner on Saturday	Larry & Mary, 555-9753 Steve & Alice, 555-1357 Ricky, 555-3434 Nancy & Bob, 555-9191 Christine	Larry & Mary to bring desert. Steve & Alice to bring hors d'oeuvres. Ricky can't come. Nancy & Bob to bring salad. Christine to bring wine.
Call painters for estimates	A-1 Painting, 555-5634 Joe's Painting, 555-2958 Paint Specialists, 555-7207	A-1 to come to house on Thursday evening. Joe's Painting to give estimate on Saturday morning. Paint Specialists doesn't do exteriors.

CHAPTER 27

Boo! It's taboo!

Takeaway Tools:

- **Identify.** Look at the behaviors you want to change.
- **Justify.** Understand your deep motivations for shifting these behaviors.
- **Examine.** Determine, for each behavior, if it's worth working on at this time in your life.
- **Balance.** Avoid the extremes of too much *and* too little. Live a balanced, happy, productive life.

Are you familiar with the Eastern concept of Yin and Yang? It's the thousands-of-years-old idea of finding your center and purpose in life by balancing opposites. Too much or too little of a good thing can become a bad thing—but by exercising self-control, we can balance the extremes and make ourselves stronger by practicing moderation.

The rest of this short chapter shows how.

Checking Your Behavior with a Taboo List

All of us engage in negative behaviors that steal time from us—or worse, put us on a path of self-destruction. The good news: when we control these destructive impulses, we prevent them from stealing our time, reduce their negative impact, and generally improve our lives.

The first step is to become aware of our negative impulses and behaviors, such as:

Sleeping too much
Sleeping too little
Eating too quickly
Eating too slowly
Exercising too much
Not exercising enough
Keeping a messy home
Obsessing over cleanliness
Purchasing unnecessary things
Not purchasing necessary things
Arguing with your partner
Not standing up to your partner

On this particular list—yours may be different—they're all either too much or too little of a good thing.

How can we take control of behaviors that negatively impact our lives? I've found it helpful to put together a Taboo List.

What is a Taboo List?

A Taboo List is not a list of the time thieves; by now, you're already bringing those under control. Rather, this list makes us aware of personal behaviors that we would like to change. In order to control these behaviors, we need to understand how and why we benefit by eliminating them, and the Taboo List is a great tool for that. Once we know—not just in our heads, but in our hearts—not just what personal behaviors we want to stop but **why** we want to stop them, we can get out from under their negative, constricting pressure on our lives.

Creating a Taboo List

Make a Taboo List with four columns:

Your personal list of behaviors you want to control.

The specific and personal reasons why you want to control those behaviors, such as:

wastes my time
hurts my relationship
makes me overweight
bad for my health

Is it worth the effort? Controlling behavior always requires effort. Based on your priorities, decide if controlling the behavior will produce results that are important to you.

How you intend to control those behaviors you've decided are worth changing—your specific action steps (leave this column blank for behaviors you've chosen not to change).

Here's a sample Taboo List:

Behavior	Why Control?	Worth Changing It?	How to Do It
don't get enough sleep	1) bad for my health 2) often too tired to be at my best	Yes - I want to be more physically active, and I want to give my best to my family.	1) Get a more comfortable mattress. 2) Stop watching late night TV.
listen to music in my car while commuting	wastes my time – could do more productive things	No – I enjoy music and it puts me in a better mood when I get to work and makes me more relaxed when I get home.	
skip lunch when busy at work	1) bad for my attitude 2) often too hungry to be at my best	Yes – I will actually get more done if I have a better attitude and am able to work at my best	1) Plan lunch according to work load – bring a lunch when I know that I am very busy. 2) Think of lunch as a reward for hard work.

Using a Taboo List

A Taboo List should be short and simple. It gets you started by identifying behaviors you want to eliminate and developing a plan to control the ones that are worth changing. You won't need to review it constantly, but you may want to revisit it periodically to see if you should add other behaviors or if your priorities have shifted.

A Taboo List is an important tool for managing your time and for improving your life. It helps you apply your priorities when deciding what personal behaviors you'd like to improve, and see the specific results you hope to achieve.

Yes, it can help you change behaviors that you don't like and that waste your time. But what might even be more important is the way it can help you see the positive aspects of some behaviors that you initially thought of as negative. When you can understand the benefits, you can accept these behaviors and stop wasting your time and energy trying to change them.

CHAPTER 28

Healthy lifestyle and success with money

Takeaway Tools:

- **Balance.** Maintain a healthy balance between work and play.
- **Appreciation.** Appreciate the power of money in your life, but don't let it rule you.
- **Plan.**Plan ahead so that your cash flow never dries up.
- **Reputation.** Everything you do, every day, builds your reputation—personally and professionally. Always treat others with kindness and respect, be true to your word, honor your commitments, and be a problem-solver.

It should be very clear by now that having money is only one ingredient in a happy life; you can be very happy even if your bank account is slim. A happy life is really built on things like surrounding yourself with people who love you, maintaining physical health, pursuing your passions, and taking time to relax and unwind—the many things that spice up your life and add flavor to your days. I've actually written other books on finding happiness.

However, since this book is about cash flow, here are a few more nuggets about how to integrate a happy lifestyle AND success with money.

The Cash Flow Secret

The secret of creating positive cash flow is to appreciate money. Respect it and understand what it can do for you. But understand that money does not own you! You're free to live your life any way you choose. Money is neither your master nor your slave; it's your friend.

Cash flow will always be an integral part of your personal and business finances; that's why it's such a powerful ally. It's a tool for your financial strength and freedom—not a barrier.

Planning is key. When you pay attention to the projected expenses and income that create your personal cash flow, you're able to take control of how, where, and when your money will flow. If you work on salary, you know exactly how much money you'll have in your bank account each month, and you can easily set budgets, put money aside to invest and save, and manage your other long-term planning goals.

While planning is easier if you have a salary or other fixed income, the rewards are often much greater when you're an entrepreneur. When you have your own business, cash flow is influenced by six major components:

Quality products or services—including excellent customer service

Market demand (people have to want what you sell—and markets can change quickly; just ask anyone who made a fortune selling typewriters, camera film, or girdles)

On-time delivery

Relationships based on trust

Methods of payment, discounts, and credit terms that are fair to both your customers and your business

Paperwork handled accurately and efficiently

When you work with vendors and customers, these suggestions will strengthen your cash flow:

Honor your commitments

Negotiate terms that are fair to everyone

Pay with credit cards to buy more time (but pay the cards back, in full, before the due date)

Pay early when it entitles you to discounts

Once you learn to maintain a healthy cash flow, you'll never run out of cash; you'll be able to purchase needed items as you need them, and you won't worry about paying bills. It's a powerful feeling to be in control of your financial health.

But don't get obsessive; this is when it's doubly important to maintain that balance and make sure you're also cultivating the other things that make you happy.

Avoid the trap of workaholism. Save time to pursue your passions…play with your children or grandchildren, your life partner, or your friends…exercise—nurture all the other parts of your life that boost your happiness.

Passive Income

When you create passive (also called residual) income streams, you earn more while working less; instead of being paid once for your time, you get paid over and over again for the value you've already provided. Examples include:

- Investment income (interest and dividends, selling off something that increases in value like an art collection or a Persian rug)
- Royalties from a book you've written or a music album you've recorded
- Sales from products you've created or financed
- Rental income from real estate

Passive income streams remove you from the direct need to constantly create cash flow, thus freeing up your time for other pursuits.

Building a healthy lifestyle and success with money relies most heavily on one thing: YOU. You must be authentic in all of your pursuits. Build your reputation on integrity, quality, accuracy, and dedication to your cause. Go into every challenge with a problem-solving attitude. Build real relationships and show genuine interest in others. And when this is the way you live your life, you'll find that people will go out of their way to do nice things for you.

You are the creator of the lifestyle you choose to live. Please use these tools to their full advantage and reap all of the benefits of this wonderful life.

CHAPTER 29

Making the world better

Takeaway Tools:

- **Tithe.** Give one-tenth of your income away.
- **Research.** Find the right charity for your business and as an individual.
- **Time.** Give your time by volunteering.
- **Leverage.** Leverage your contribution by giving goods or services.

This may be the most surprising secret to creating a successful cash flow—give it away! One of the biggest benefits of money is that you can use it for the greater good. When you channel the power of your cash flow to make the world a better place, the floodgates open, and your cash becomes even more powerful as you attract more of it.

Interestingly enough, many prosperity experts recommend giving away a significant portion of your wealth—and many of the richest people of all time, from Andrew Carnegie 100 years ago to Warren Buffett and Bill and Melinda Gates today, have given great fortunes to charity.

Give freely; give often. When you give with warm hands and a warm heart, you create money success. It's amazingly powerful to help others when they need it the most. They in turn will have a chance to pay it forward, and your gift will spiral the global economy toward health. So spread the wealth! It will come back to you in countless ways.

The Principle of Tithing

Originally a traditional Jewish practice, tithing—giving one-tenth of your earnings away—has since been adopted by many other religious groups, organizations, and individuals. This planned act of charity may sometimes feel like a sacrifice—especially when you're just starting a business—but it's incredibly powerful, both in the direct benefit to the communities that receive it, and to your own financial well-being.

People who tithe honor their community and their world by giving a substantial portion of their wealth away. Tithing is also a way to express gratitude for the gift of success—and sincere gratitude has a nifty way of bringing more blessings.

Finding the Right Charity

Whatever amount you decide to give, you need to choose where to contribute. Spend some time thinking about organizations you would like to support. Look for:

Alignment with your values.

A high percentage of the budget funding the actual betterment work, rather than for administration or marketing.

Clear and visible results so you know your money makes a real difference.

You may decide to choose one charity (or set of charities) for your business contributions and another for your personal contributions. That's great! And if your choice for personal contributions may be controversial or uncomfortable for some of your customers, it's also a wise business move to separate the two streams.

Deciding on a charity is ultimately a very personal decision. People often choose organizations based on events in their lives or times when they've received assistance. You may have a parent who is a cancer survivor, and so you choose to support cancer research. Or maybe the Boys and Girls Club was instrumental in helping you grow as a young child, so you choose to help that organization help more kids. You may want to give locally to directly help your community, or you may be more interested in contributing to global concerns. You can choose to give a large amount to one or two charities, smaller donations to many more organizations, or to fund an umbrella agency (such as United Way, Green America, or Haymarket People's Fund) that has already vetted causes to support.

Your choice of charities is completely up to you, and it can change as often as you like. Many businesses choose a different charity or group of charities to support every year. There are thousands of opportunities and places to give; spend some time thinking about how and where you would like to make a difference, and then channel your cash flow in that direction.

Donate Your Time or Your Goods and Services

Not all of your contributions need to be monetary; your time and your products or services are equally valuable. When you find an organization that you feel passionate about, consider volunteering. As you become personally involved in making the world a better place, your happiness and connection with the world around you increase exponentially. The benefits of volunteering and simple good deeds are incalculable.

And while it's not the reason to volunteer, an added benefit is that people in important positions get to know you and your business, build relationships with you, and see you in action as a skilled and passionate advocate for their cause; this can come back to you many times over in new business and opportunities.

Another great way to make a difference through your business is to donate goods or services. Leverage your monetary contributions by giving away your products either for the organization to use directly, or as fundraisers. These gifts can be extremely valuable to the right organization—and great publicity as well as tax deductions for you. These donations show very tangibly that your organization cares about the community and is actively involved.

It's not all about you. We're in this together, and it's important to help each other out along the way. Cash flow is a global experience. Rather than holding tight to your money and damming up the flow, create healthy new streams and make the world a better place by adding to the current of compassion in our world.

FINALE

On March 19, 2006, I began to live on my own for the very first time in my adult life.

I fell in love with my small condo and I felt so liberated and free and comfortable.

The space and the freedom lead me to the personal changes that I'm thrilled to share with you. I became a freelance journalist, went back to school to study human behavior and literature, and began to write books —sharing the wisdom I've drawn from my life challenges and the success formulas I've developed. I began to spend a lot more time writing and coaching people in the areas I excelled in (letting go, facing the change and move forward with lightness).

I made new friends; I connected with new people from all over the world. I started to live my life in Technicolor and at the same time I became even more productive. I felt fulfilled and blessed; I loved my new life!

2006 represented the foundation and the blueprint to my new life; although everything I'd ever done led me to this place, 2006 marked the beginning. The move contributed to my conscious change and to this deeply meaningful and oh-so-satisfying mindset. In other words, leaving my third husband gave birth to the cash flow and to my happy life.

So much can evolve from starting from nothing and embracing the No's in our lives; even when life events seem out of our control we can convert them to something positive and desirable.

I must add one thing here of great importance. My Grandfather whom I never met was educated in law back in Europe, Germany. HE was a land owner and he pursued the title of Consulting in Negotiations and Business Relationships. People born in the city where Mom grew up shared with me various stories about Grandpa; his expertise and his accomplishments. He had a voice and he was respected by everyone and very much looked up to and a man of power and great charisma. My Grandma whom I also never met was conducting lectures every week on Sabbath after the prayers on personal relationships, children (she gave birth to 16) emotional challenges and the pursuit of peace of mind and personal contentment. I remember back when I was a little girl Mom's stories and neighbor's from her town about my Grandma. They said that when she spoke she would lift everyone's spirit and raise their passion for life. The ladies were looking forward to her lectures on Sabbath and never missed a day. In Hebrew there is the word SCHINA, (means the light of God touching). According to the stories and events I heard; when Grandma walked into the Synagogue there was an aura about her, everyone looked and felt her presence like the Schina was entering the place. How delightful. Grandma never raised her voice but her appearance had a huge impact on people around her.

Indeed it's all turning into a full circle. How delightful!!!

A big WHAA, and a big moment here. How amazing.

Year—1912— and moving fast forward 100 years later I am continuing their legacy with a deep passion and direction I wasn't asked to do or instructed to follow their path. It's a path meant to be shared and exposed today.

Mom is the 16th child and she inherited their life contentment, character, trust, hope and strength so here we are finding out that the wisdom lies in embracing the life we have, cherish it and make it meaningful and juggle it skillfully; connect the heart and the mind and the art of negotiating is the secret.

I wish you a great life, beyond your wildest dreams.

Please write to me and tell me how things work out for you:
ana@cashflowmastery.com

About Ana Weber... Business "Rainmaker," Writer, Speaker, 360 Degree Lifestyle Leadership Expert, and Philanthropist – founder of The DOXA method and Grow Your Cash Flow

Ana Weber's methods of teaching and empowering are exceptionally successful. In the 360 Degrees of Success workshop, Ana introduces to us the 5 essential elements, and empowers us to reach business success and personal happiness. Ana has implemented "THE DOXA METHOD" for over 26 years in the corporate world throughout her management and leadership positions: CFO, CEO, VP of Sales for a wide range of industries such as: medical devices, hospitality, architectural designs (The Smithsonian Institute) automotive, Porsche Race Car Division, apparel industry, and washers manufacturing for the trucking industry. In addition to her many decades of business experience, Ana has achieved success in multiple parallel careers—as a writer, speaker, personal and business/professional expert, and workshop leader.

Speaker and hosting workshops:

Ana's recent presentations include Canyon Ranch, Avalon European River Cruises University of Delaware, Cal Poly, San Luis Obispo, High Point University, Harvard Business Expert Forum, West Point Military Academy, Universal Music, London. TM forum Digital Live, Nice France, ECA 360 fitness N.Y., New York University, Best You, Lincoln Experience Center, One Woman Fearless, Hay House Live, Toronto, Global Woman Club, Los Angeles, PEO Non Profit for women college funds and scholarships, West Cal Academy.

Ana's upcoming book "Grow Your Cash Flow" and 360 Degrees of Success worksheets and tips are endorsed by board members of the United Nations.

Best-selling books by Ana Weber (Ana published a total of 17 books) courses, Workshops the founder of the CHANGE $ GAME

The DOXA METHOD

Passion Spirit Purpose

Companion to Passion Spirit Purpose (workbook)

360 Degrees of Success
Grow Your Cash Flow

Education:

BA International Business-University of Tel Aviv
Ashworth University Masters of Business Administration
Continued education Philosophy Ph.D Oxford University, England
Additional certification with IPEC – CPC and Master Practitioner

Philanthropy:

UNICEF, Global Woman Club, One Woman Fearless and The United Nations bazaar club.

Made in United States
Cleveland, OH
05 November 2026

47678354R00084